CONTROLLING OUR DESTINY

CONTROLLING OUR DESTINY

A BOARD MEMBER'S VIEW OF DEAF PRESIDENT NOW

Philip W. Bravin

Gallaudet University Press
Washington, DC

Gallaudet University Press
Washington, DC 20002
http://gupress.gallaudet.edu

ISBN 978-1-944838-71-3 (paperback)
ISBN 978-1-944838-73-7 (ebook)

Library of Congress Cataloging-in-Publication Data

Names: Bravin, Philip W., author.
Title: Controlling our destiny: a board member's view of Deaf President
   Now / Philip W. Bravin.
Description: Washington, DC: Gallaudet University Press, [2020] | Includes
   bibliographical references. | Summary: "An insider's view of the events
   that lead up to one of the most crucial moments in American deaf
   history: the 1988 Deaf President Now (DPN) protests at Gallaudet
   University"— Provided by publisher.
Identifiers: LCCN 2020030842 (print) | LCCN 2020030843 (ebook) | ISBN
   9781944838713 (paperback ; alk. paper) | ISBN 9781944838737 (ebook)
Subjects: LCSH: Gallaudet University—Student strike, 1988. | Gallaudet
   University—Presidents. | College presidents—Selection and
   appointment—United States. | Student strikes—Washington (D.C.) |
   Deaf—Education (Higher)—United States.
Classification: LCC HV2561.W18 G327 2020 (print) | LCC
   HV2561.W18 (ebook) | DDC 378.753—dc23
LC record available at https://lccn.loc.gov/2020030842
LC ebook record available at https://lccn.loc.gov/2020030843

Cover design by Eric C. Wilder.

To Judith, my rock
To Jeff, Deb, and Seth, my pebbles
To my grandchildren, my grains of sand
To Vermont, our solitude

Contents

Foreword   ix
I. King Jordan

Preface   xv

Acknowledgments   xix

Introduction   xxv

PART ONE: THE SEARCH FOR A NEW PRESIDENT   1

1 Remembering 170 Years of Oppression   3

2 From Kendall Green to the Work World
and Back to My Alma Mater   7

3 Setting the Presidential Precedent:
1864–1983   11

4 My Initial Years on the Board of Trustees
(1981–1986)   16

5 Laying the Foundation for the Search   29

6 Starting the Engines: The Search Begins   41

7 Narrowing Down the Pool   54

8 The Interviews   58

9 Selecting the President amid Mounting
Public Pressure   71

PART TWO: THE WEEK THE WORLD HEARD GALLAUDET   83

1 The Finale that Never Was a Finale:
March 5–6   85

2 Monday, March 7   100

3 Tuesday, March 8   110

4 Wednesday, March 9   113

5 Thursday, March 10   121
6 Friday, March 11   124
7 Saturday, March 12   128
8 Sunday, March 13   131
9 Monday, March 14   149

EPILOGUE   157

SUPPLEMENTAL MATERIALS   175
   Notable Quotes about DPN   177
   Controlling Our Destiny:
       An Unpublished Paper   183
   Cast of Characters   185
   Deaf President Now! A Ballad
       by Robert F. Panara   188
   You Have to Be Deaf to Understand
       by Willard J. Madsen   192
   The Dr. Edward C. Merrill Jr. Papers   195

Bibliography   221
About the Author   225

Foreword

I. King Jordan

In *Controlling Our Destiny*, Philip W. Bravin describes in great detail, and in close to chronological order, what happened throughout the search for Gallaudet's seventh president during a momentous week in March of 1988. Phil details the discussions and decisions made by the search committee and the board, as they narrowed the pool of candidates and finally voted to name a hearing person, Dr. Elisabeth Zinser, as president, and his experiences during the weeklong protest after that.

At the end of the week, after Dr. Zinser had resigned and the board voted to name me Gallaudet's eighth president and first deaf president, the Deaf President Now (DPN) movement, which had succeeded beyond what anyone could have envisioned, was, for all intents and purposes, over.

On the morning of Monday, March 14, Gallaudet's campus was peaceful but energized. Students and faculty sensed that the world had changed for deaf people, and to ensure that the changes going forward continued to be positive, there needed to be support for the first deaf president.

Early that morning, Greg Hlibok, who was elected president of the Gallaudet Student Body Government (SBG) shortly before DPN; Phil Bravin, who was elected chair of the Gallaudet board the day before; and myself, who was appointed president at the same time, met in my office in the Edward Miner Gallaudet (EMG) building. As we chatted informally to start the meeting, Greg pointed out that it was surely the first time in the 124-year history of the university that the SBG president, the university president, and the chair of the board could communicate clearly and easily without the need for an American Sign Language (ASL) interpreter. That simple fact hit the three of us like a ton of bricks. It was simple, yes, but it was profound beyond anything else we could have said.

Much of what Phil includes in this book is new to me and will be new even to people who were deeply involved with the activities of DPN during the week of March 6–13, 1988. At several points, he notes how strongly he felt about the confidentiality of the search and how proud he was that things remained confidential throughout. As someone who had a real interest in what might have been happening during the search and who knew several members of the search committee, I never had a hint of any "inside information." Phil's almost obsessive attention to confidentiality and the outstanding support provided to him and the committee by Lil Holt could be used as a template for how to conduct a presidential search. Congratulations to him, Lil, and to each member of the committee for that.

As Phil notes, he and I were not close before DPN. Our paths had crossed, and we knew each other, but when he was on campus for board meetings I was either an academic department chair or dean, so there was a necessary separation between us. While we certainly became much closer after I was appointed president and he was elected chair, during the search and the protest, many things were happening in our lives at the same time about which neither of us knew.

Phil describes well the phone call he made to me on Sunday, March 6, in which he informed me that I had not been selected as president. For those who read this book but who have not experienced using a teletypewriter (TTY) to make phone calls, this information will not carry the same emotion as it will for those of us who could make phone calls only on a TTY. Turn-taking on a TTY call happens when the person who is typing ends what they say by typing "GA," which means *go ahead*. That's both an invitation for the other person to begin typing and the message that the first person is done. GA says,

"Okay, I'm done; your turn." To end a call, someone types "SK," which means *stop keying*. If the first person types SK and the second person has nothing more to say, he or she types back "SKSK," and the call is finished. If I had a stopwatch during the call Phil made to me to let me know that I had not been selected, the entire thing would have lasted about thirty seconds. It was not a pleasant call for either of us.

I had been interviewed by the board earlier that day. Confidentiality was so much of a concern that the university sent a car and driver to my home in Silver Spring to pick me up and drive me to where the interview was to take place. I asked the driver if he could tell my wife where we were going, so that she could meet me or pick me up after the interview was done. He said no. He would bring me back home afterward.

The interview was not a pleasant experience for me; however, I thought I did a good job of presenting myself as a candidate who could immediately assume the role of president. It was not a good experience for two reasons, both of which are alluded to in this book. First, the room was not configured well for communicating in sign language. The room was long and narrow, and it was almost impossible to see who was asking a question. It must have been very difficult for the interpreters, and it was extremely difficult for me. Second, and more important (and also alluded to by Phil), were all the follow-up questions put to me by Jane Spilman, chair of the board. After nearly every response I made to a question, she would follow up with another that frequently took issue with my reply. I left the room after my two-hour interview with the sense that she had been borderline hostile to me. After reading Phil's narrative and the comments made to Jane by another deaf board member, I now think that it was more than borderline.

I mentioned earlier that Phil and I were both dealing with DPN at the same time but in different places and in different ways. A few things that he doesn't know or write about are important, I think.

On Wednesday, March 9, Catherine Ingold, Gallaudet's provost and my immediate supervisor, called and asked to meet with me. At the same time, Phil had been called by Jane Spilman to meet with her. Catherine Ingold told me that she had been meeting with Elisabeth Zinser, who had asked her to arrange a meeting with the student leaders. I was asked to help make that happen.

I went to the campus and met with the DPN Council in Ole Jim and presented her request. After a long discussion with a lot of back and forth, the students agreed that they would meet with her, but they would not meet her on campus. My memory is that someone said, "She cannot set foot on campus."

Arrangements were made to meet at a local motel on New York Avenue. Dr. Zinser and I were taken to the motel by a Gallaudet driver, and when we got there, we went to a regular, small motel room furnished with a bed, desk, and chair. There were seven of us in the room. The four student leaders, an ASL interpreter, Dr. Zinser, and me. As you can imagine, it was crowded. The students were very polite, friendly, and attentive, but they were absolutely resolute in their position that their four demands—(1) Gallaudet must have a deaf president; (2) Jane Spilman must resign from the board; (3) at least 51 percent of the board must be deaf; and (4) there would be no reprisals for protesting students or dissenting faculty—would need to be met before the protest would end and the campus would reopen. They said that they respected her and her good work, but that she was not the right person to lead a university for deaf people.

Dr. Zinser tried her best to soften their position but failed, so we left the meeting and got back into the car. Unknown to me, we were driving from the motel to the National Press Club, where there would be a major press conference during which the board would reaffirm their support for Dr. Zinser. For the entire drive, Dr. Zinser talked on her phone. I had no idea to whom she was speaking or what she was talking about, but as

I sat there, I realized that she simply didn't have a clue as to the communication needs of or respect for a deaf person.

At the press conference, I was rushed to the podium and told to show my support for the board's decision. At the time, I did exactly what Phil and the other members of the board had done: I affirmed that the board had the authority and responsibility to elect the president, which they had done, and as a university administrator, I supported that.

Immediately after the press conference, I was driven back to Gallaudet and arrived just as a meeting of the faculty was concluding. In that meeting, they had voted to support the student protest. One of the faculty leaders, Dr. Harvey Goodstein, saw me, took me aside, and gave me a strong and emotional hug. He told me that he disagreed with me completely but understood why I had said what I did at the press conference. His positivity toward me meant a great deal.

That evening, at home, I got a phone call from Dr. Edward Merrill, Gallaudet's fourth president. Dr. Merrill also knew of the press conference, and he encouraged me to stop trying to think like an administrator and instead just listen to my heart and act on that. That call meant a lot to me, and when I hung up, I said to my wife, he's absolutely right. I need to remember that I am a dean, but I am also deaf. I am D-E-A-N only as long as my supervisor agrees I should remain in that position, but I am D-E-A-F for the rest of my life.

The next day, Thursday, March 10, my wife and I met with the DPN Council and told them that I was ready to make a public statement in support of the protest. We sat and I drafted a statement, and the council arranged an impromptu press conference on the steps of Chapel Hall, where I said that the student demands were reasonable and appropriate and that they had my full support.

Here are a few final thoughts I will share before I conclude. First, and very important, DPN was much more than a protest. It began as a protest, to be sure, but it quickly became a revolution, a revolution that forced the Gallaudet University Board of Trustees to recognize the rights and abilities of people who are deaf. That revolution continues and would not have been possible without the protest.

Second, after I became president of Gallaudet, I had many opportunities to spend time with Elisabeth Zinser. She is a lovely woman and a very able academic administrator. But she, just like most of the hearing members of the board, was utterly ignorant about deafness. I believe that she knows that now. She was simply the wrong person in the wrong place at the wrong time.

Third, I had the opportunity to have dinner and talk with Jane Bassett Spilman after I had been president for some time. She was very pleasant and clearly wanted me to be a successful president. She assured me that she never made that infamous statement, "Deaf people are not ready to function in a hearing world" on the night Zinser was selected as Gallaudet's president, and she understood how significant that misunderstanding was in the entire scheme of things.

Finally, Phil made a second phone call to me on the TTY on March 13, which was much more positive and friendlier than the one made to me on March 6. He and I became good friends and had pretty much a perfect board chair–president relationship. I thank him for that.

In this book, Phil Bravin does a very good job of presenting an insider's view, and I would guess that much of what he says here he is saying openly for the first time. Phil Bravin shows how just a lack of knowledge about how to communicate with deaf people helped lead to a revolution that continues to bring positive attention to deaf people and all people with disabilities. I congratulate him on his outstanding work with the search committee, with the board, and with this book.

Preface

> *We hold these truths to be self-evident, that all men are created equal, that they are endowed by their Creator with certain unalienable Rights, that among these are Life, Liberty and the Pursuit of Happiness.*
>
> *United States Declaration of Independence*

This is a real-life account of how a small group of people helped achieve what our forefathers intended as our rights as citizens of this country. It took more than 171 years from the time the first deaf child entered school in the United States to the time of the Deaf President Now (DPN) movement at Gallaudet University in 1988. In 1817, that first deaf student, Alice Cogswell, initiated the recognition in the United States that deaf people could be educated. However, until 1988, the mantle of deaf leadership at Gallaudet was never recognized for deaf people. When the Declaration of Independence was written, our forefathers intended that everyone who was considered to be a citizen at that time, deaf or hearing, be given the same opportunities and privileges.

Other deaf people have written books and stories of the DPN movement from different perspectives—as a protester, a sociologist, or a participant—but none have been written from an insider's point of view. This book is my attempt to tell that story.

Soon after the events of March 1988, people began to ask me to write an account from my point of view as a member of the Gallaudet University Board of Trustees. I had kept documents of most of the events, and although not perfectly dated or organized, I had enough to create a historical narrative of the events leading up to and following the protest. However, it has taken me thirty years to put my thoughts down on paper, mainly due to interruptions and distractions, both personal and professional. It also was not possible for me to share the details of very sensitive situations back then. As I pondered writing the book, I realized that the time lapse had created an opportunity for me to be more open about my DPN experiences. My professional concerns of thirty years ago do not exist today. Furthermore, many of the board members involved in DPN have passed on to the Great Beyond.

This is not only a book for the deaf community but also a book for other stakeholders, including boards of trustees of other colleges and universities, for I have tried to provide a sense of how a board conducts a presidential search. Very little has been published about how boards actually perform a search, mainly because certain meetings, especially executive sessions, are closed to everyone except board members. The minutes of such meetings contain highly sensitive information and are usually sealed, seen only by those who have a right or need to know. As a result, most people outside this small group do not fully comprehend nor appreciate how a search is conducted. In this book, I reveal the activities of such sessions, using only information that has historical significance to explain better the various events that led to the DPN movement. I did not make this decision lightly, for I did not want to establish a precedent for the Gallaudet University Board of Trustees or for other boards as well. The sanctity of executive sessions needs to be respected and protected.

The DPN movement was a watershed event for the deaf community. It allowed the general public to understand better and appreciate the cultural and historical nuances of the deaf community, which contributed to the protest. More importantly, many young deaf children and their stakeholders today do not have any information or knowledge of the movement from a historical perspective. I also wanted to write this book so that the deaf community will have a document memorializing the circumstances and reasons the movement took place. My writing may contain some errors or omissions of detail. They may be inadvertent, due to missing documents, or done on purpose. The goal was to tell the story, as I saw it, without compromising personal or sensitive matters.

It is my sincere hope that after reading this book, readers will appreciate how DPN was the realization of our birthright as citizens of the United States.

Acknowledgments

With sincere thanks . . .

In March 1988, the students of Gallaudet University locked down the campus over the selection of a new, hearing president. The week that followed became known as Deaf President Now (DPN), and it brought changes in the governance of the university, which few dreamed were possible. At the time, I was a member of the Gallaudet University Board of Trustees, which gave me an insider's view of the week's events.

In the years following DPN, family members and friends encouraged me to put my thoughts and observations about DPN on paper. Some wanted me to reveal everything that happened behind the scenes; some advised me to be careful; and others asked me to keep sensitive disclosures to a minimum. In the beginning, I struggled with myself over whether I should tell this story, but after several years, I realized that I was in a unique position to share information and observations that only a few other people could. Not to share my observations would have left a gap in deaf history; yet, I wanted to be sure that I could present a balanced view.

Two key leaders in the deaf community gave me the impetus to forge ahead and tell the story as I saw fit. Merv Garretson, a well-known leader in the deaf community, Gallaudet faculty member, administrator, and a former board colleague, whom I visited at his home in Florida a few months before his passing, told me, "Phil, you must tell this story. The deaf community and the world need to know what happened. Without what you have seen and gone through, we would have half the story, and that won't be fair to history." He put his frail hand on my shoulder and said, "Do it, not for me, but for everyone." Jack

Gannon, another great Gallaudetian and author, sat across from me at a table and said, "I have written my version of the Deaf President Now movement, but it won't be complete without your version. Go ahead and do it." The rest is history, though it took several years of research, writing, and countless trips to the Gallaudet Archives. Mike Olson, Gallaudet's senior archivist, graciously opened the files to allow me to find information that existed only in the archives. Before I accessed the DPN materials, I sought permission from the board of trustees in March 2013 to read the minutes of meetings held during the time period I served on the board, both as a member and as its chair. I wanted to be sure my telling was based on facts, not just my recollections. The response I got was that there was a provision in the minutes that the DPN materials be sealed for fifty years. After I asked for and received a copy of that provision, I read that "Phil Bravin, as chair, recommended to the Board that the records be sealed for fifty years"! I then went back to the board to ask for access with the understanding that I would use my best judgment to not reveal certain sensitive matters. To my great relief, the board granted my request, for which I am truly grateful.

In any university, no one should overlook the staff who support the president and the board. I have had the good fortune of working with wonderful people, like Lil Holt, Sheila Deane, Bette Martin, and Sue Russell, who performed so admirably in their respective capacities. I also want to acknowledge the work of Pat Thompson, Julia Pitt, Maryte Dyess, the president's office, and Gallaudet's campus security officers, who worked so hard to ensure my safety during and following DPN in my duties as a board member and chair, not to mention their taking care of some of my transportation needs along with the Department of Transportation on campus.

Like a marathon runner, I hit "the wall" trying to finish the last mile of the book. I sought help from my good friend Steve Baldwin, who has authored several books and is a Gallaudet alum. Steve jumped in and gave me the final push I needed to get past the wall, for which I am very grateful.

I would also like to thank Patrick Harris of Gallaudet's Video Services Department, who was able to extract stills from very fragile video footage taken during DPN; it required some delicate work. A number of the pictures haven't been seen until now.

I extend my gratitude to the people at Gallaudet University Press: Katie Lee, Deirdre Mullervy, and Angela Leppig. Special thanks to Ivey Pittle Wallace, who originally reviewed my manuscript and worked over several years to get this book ready for publication. Her thoughts, advice, and foresight were invaluable to me as a first-time author. Ivey, in her retirement, stepped up to shepherd this to completion.

While I was working on the book, I also had a full-time job as vice president of product strategy and innovation at ZVRS/ Purple, a video relay company. My chief executive officer (CEO), Sherri Turpin, gave me the necessary resources, support and, most importantly, the time that I needed to complete the book. My colleagues at ZVRS/Purple gave me unending support and cheered me on to the end.

My partner during the search process was Nancy Archer-Martin, who is a well-respected search professional. She came on board in the middle of the search process and helped me navigate the sometimes-rocky course by providing support and counsel. Myra Peabody Gossens, a public relations professional, was brought in after the end of the search, and she stayed with us for a while to work on public relations and board relations efforts, which were critically needed. Nancy and Myra, although in the background, were invaluable to Gallaudet and me.

American Sign Language (ASL) interpreters usually remain nameless, but they facilitated most of my communication during the entire search and DPN. While many interpreters were involved, I want to give particular recognition to Janet

Bailey, Sheila Deane, Earl Elkins, and Jan Nishimura. They worked countless hours, including at odd times and over weekends, to ensure that communication between deaf people and hearing people was accurate and reflected the tonal and emotional nuances that are essential for a deaf person. My sincere appreciation goes out to Nancy, Myra, Janet, Sheila, Earl, and Jan.

I want to thank the four student leaders—Bridgetta Bourne-Firl, Jerry Covell, Greg Hlibok, and Tim Rarus—for their steadfastness during the movement and for showing us that deaf people can control their destiny. Without them, the world today would not be as bright for deaf people. The deaf community had the vital role of supporting the students and DPN leaders, and their contribution should not be overlooked. I also want to acknowledge President I. King Jordan's efforts in making a world of difference for deaf people everywhere.

My colleagues on the board before, during, and after DPN need to be recognized and appreciated. The board members gave a lot of their time and energy to advance the mission of Gallaudet. My deaf and hard of hearing colleagues on the board read the situation perfectly—the time was right for a deaf president. The actions of the hearing members of the board during the final week of the DPN movement was an unintentional anomaly. They took the issue seriously and dealt with it as best as they could. Going forward, it should be noted that hearing people are important partners in serving the deaf community in various capacities. We are coequals in society and can also work together to make the world a better place for deaf people everywhere.

Finally, and most appreciatively, I am thankful to the members of my immediate and extended family, especially my wife Judy. She gave up time and weekends to allow me to attend to writing. We missed some hiking and snowshoeing opportunities that I can now make up to her. Judy has always been there for me prior, during, and after the DPN movement and then during the development of the manuscript, gently reminding me to keep going. That was a difficult task, but she persevered. I love you, Judy. My three children, Jeff, Deb, and Seth, and their families, were also my supporters; they reviewed the manuscript at several stages and provided me with invaluable feedback, sprinkled with love. My aunt Miriam Zadek, who is also a budding author, has always kept track of my progress and given me encouragement, which was needed at times. My little sister, Sherry Bravin Duhon, was always there, making sure her big brother was on track during the movement and since then. Because she was a Gallaudet employee during DPN, we were able to separate our familial and professional lives. With respect and thanks to Sherry, she never attempted to ask me to divulge any information related to the presidential search or my tenure on the board. She was fully cognizant of my role and never crossed that line. Many of my close friends kept checking on my progress—that in and of itself was their deed of encouragement.

Now the story can be told, with sincere thanks to everyone I mentioned and with appreciation and apologies to those I overlooked.

Introduction

This story begins on August 25, 1987. I was in Vermont with my family at our A-frame chalet among the trees for our usual late August vacation before the September craze began. My wife, Judy, a librarian at the New York School for the Deaf, was preparing to go back to school, as were our children—Jeff was a freshman at Gallaudet University, and Deb and Seth were high school students at the Lexington School for the Deaf.

Vermont in late August is always special; the weather starts to turn a bit cool, and the tips of the leaves begin to change colors. Evenings are usually brisk, and the air smells of pine when we go out for a walk under the moon. When there's no moon, the neighborhood is extremely dark, for there are no streetlights on our dirt road. Trebo Road has been there for more than a hundred years, almost wholly dirt for its six-mile length. Over half of the roads in Vermont are dirt, and they have served us well except during the mud season when the snow melts, and the dirt doesn't seem to be able to absorb so much water at a given time. The mud stays with us for about a month or so. Washing cars is useless at that time of the year.

One afternoon, while resting in our great room, the lamp next to the phone flashed, letting us know we were getting a call. We then had a TTY, a portable teletypewriter—a smaller version of the bulky machines the Army, Western Union, and the press used in the 1940s and 1950s to send and receive printed messages. Our device had an alphanumeric display with a small printer to print the messages we typed back and forth. This was how deaf people were able to communicate over the phone in those days.

It was a call from our daughter, Deb, who was staying in New York. She indicated that the office of the president at Gallaudet had been trying to reach me—they didn't have our Vermont number, which we did not freely give away. Having been a trustee for the past six years, I knew that such phone calls between board meetings from the president or the board chair were rare and usually for a good or a crisis-related reason. I then called the president's office back and was put on hold while they got Dr. Jerry C. Lee, the then president of Gallaudet, on the phone. After some pleasantries, Dr. Lee indicated that he was stepping down as president of Gallaudet later in the year. When I asked Jerry what his plans were after stepping down, he indicated that he was going to work for Robert Spilman, who was the CEO of Bassett Furniture. That took me aback (and puzzled me) as the then chair of the Gallaudet University Board of Trustees at that time was Jane Bassett Spilman, the wife of Robert Spilman. This was an unusual set of circumstances, and after congratulations and best wishes from me, Jerry put Jane on the phone, and I indicated to Jane that I was sorry to see Jerry go. This news was a stunner—Dr. Lee, in his short tenure of nearly four years, had performed admirably for the university, and there was no indication whatsoever that he was contemplating such an action.

Jane opened with the usual greetings, as she was a very well-poised and down-to-earth person. One's first impression of Jane was that she was a woman of dignity—she was always well dressed and well-coiffed. A greeting hug from her was always genuine and accompanied by a contagious smile. Jane had joined the board shortly before me in 1981, and she commanded respect and made us do our work very well. I was relatively young to be a board member then, being forty-two years old, but my youth in relation to her age—she was probably ten to fifteen years older than I was at that time—did not mean a thing. She obviously, for whatever reason, saw me as a useful board member and put me on several missions for the university before that phone call.

As Jane's middle name indicates, she was part of the Bassett furniture empire that her father founded. Up to that time, she had never mixed the business with university matters. The call from Dr. Lee that day changed everything. Sure enough, Jane wanted to talk to me about another mission.

Jane asked me point blank, "Would you consider serving as chair of the search committee to find the best person to replace Dr. Lee as president of Gallaudet?" This question took me aback because not in a hundred years would I expect to be called to duty in such an honorable and extremely sensitive situation. I told Jane, "Even though I am humbled and flattered by your request, I would ask that you give me some time to think about this—I want to do it, but I want to think about it before giving this my full commitment." I was fully aware of the enormous responsibility that would befall me—both personally and publicly.

I shared the news with Judy, and she, being a Gallaudet alum like me, felt so proud of me. At the same time, she was fully aware of the daunting task that lay ahead of me. Why so huge and significant, one may ask? The answer lies in the role Gallaudet University plays in the deaf community. Gallaudet is considered a "mecca" for deaf people. It could well be called the Harvard of the deaf world. Many of its graduates have assumed leadership positions in the deaf community, as well as in the larger hearing society. I consider myself a proud Gallaudetian, so to be called to duty to find a president for Gallaudet was a huge undertaking and a humbling responsibility.

Thankfully, I was in Vermont when I received the call from Jane Spilman. Vermont is quiet, even for a deaf person. During most of the year, we lived in Pelham Manor, New York, a suburb of New York City in Westchester County. We would go to our home in Vermont to recharge our batteries and clear our minds. The tranquility afforded me the space to think thoroughly through the challenge I had been offered.

There were many elements to the challenge—political, emotional, and practical. Being the mecca Gallaudet is, the entire deaf community would be watching and monitoring the search with a close eye. Up to that day in August 1987, Gallaudet had had six presidents—none of whom were deaf, in contrast to Gallaudet's mission to produce deaf leaders, and its board of trustees had never had a majority of deaf members. This situation created the expectation that this time, Gallaudet would get a deaf president. In 1950, there were no deaf people with PhDs. By 1987, we had more than twenty-five with earned doctorates and other professional degrees, and this created part of the pool from which to choose the first deaf president. The dilemma was whether Gallaudet should focus only on deaf candidates or find the best person regardless of whether that person was deaf or hearing. This choice would be the challenge before me.

A few days later, I called Jane back on the TTY to tell her I was willing to chair the search committee with some conditions, to which she readily agreed. One was that I would have full control of the process and that she, as chair, would be in a consultative role. The other was that I would have the full prerogative of selecting members of the committee from Gallaudet's various constituencies to serve on the search committee. Still, the majority of the committee would be composed of board members. That was the deal we struck. Finally, I asked if Lil Holt, the board support liaison, could be my support person. "Sure," said Jane without hesitation. That was a big catch. If anyone could keep me straight, considering the weak paperwork and organizational skills I had, it would be Lil. As it turned out, Lil and I made an excellent team for the duration of the search and beyond. Bless her. The search process was bound to be a logistical nightmare, and everything had to be done correctly, with no missed heartbeats. My life has never been the same since.

PART ONE

THE SEARCH FOR
A NEW PRESIDENT

1

Remembering 170 Years of Oppression

One may ask why the deaf community was so invested in the outcome of Gallaudet's presidential search. To answer this question, we need to understand how the deaf community in America came to be and what it experienced up until 1988. Before 1817, there were a few areas in New England with a higher-than-average number of deaf people. These small groups had little, if any, awareness of each other. This began to change in 1817, when the first permanent school for deaf children opened in Hartford, Connecticut. The seeds of the school were sown by several well-to-do families who wanted to educate their deaf children but did not want to send them to the established schools overseas. One of the parents, Dr. Mason Fitch Cogswell, had a neighbor who had taken an interest in Cogswell's daughter Alice, who was deaf. This man, the Reverend Thomas Hopkins Gallaudet, had tried to teach Alice to read. Gallaudet and Cogswell discussed the need to establish a school for deaf children in America, and they began to raise funds to send someone to Europe to learn the teaching methods used there. With support from other parents, they raised enough money to send Gallaudet on this mission in 1815.

Gallaudet first went to London, where he found that the directors of the school were unwilling to share their methods, which focused on speech and speechreading, unless Gallaudet agreed to stay for several years. He had not intended to stay that long and was about to decline the offer when, by chance, he attended a public lecture in London by two former pupils and the director, Abbe Sicard, of the school for the deaf in Paris. These men used sign language to communicate, and when they took questions from the audience, they wrote their responses on a chalkboard. Gallaudet was very impressed, so he asked the Paris school's director if he could come and observe the classes.

After spending almost a year at the Paris school, Gallaudet became convinced that sign language was the means to educate and communicate with deaf people. This approach, called the *manual method*, was used throughout France, unlike in England, where the school used the *oral method* and forbade the use of sign language. When Gallaudet decided to return to Connecticut, Laurent Clerc, a deaf teacher, volunteered to go with him to start the school in America.

In June 1816, Gallaudet and Clerc boarded the *Mary Augusta* for the voyage to America. They used the time on the trip to improve their language skills—Gallaudet in sign language and Clerc in English. After returning to Hartford, they worked with Cogswell to raise money for their school, and their efforts resulted in the establishment, in April 1817, of what is known today as the American School for the Deaf.[1] Alice Cogswell was one of the first students at the new school, and Clerc was the first teacher. Gallaudet, Cogswell, and Clerc have gone down in deaf history and culture as the keystones of the deaf community in America.

In the early to mid-1800s, many graduates of the American School for the Deaf became teachers at the school. Others went to other states to set up and teach at similar schools for the deaf. By 1860, about 40 percent of the teachers in schools for the deaf in America were themselves deaf. This period also saw the growth of the deaf community in America. Children at the residential schools developed lifelong friendships with their classmates and, in the process, formed a cohesive community centered around their shared language and culture.

The opening of the National Deaf-Mute College (now Gallaudet University) in 1864 was a watershed moment for

---

1. Harlan Lane, *When the Mind Hears* (New York: Random House, 1984), 206.

the deaf community. For the first time, deaf people could receive higher education in their language. Incidentally, the first president of the college was none other than Edward Miner Gallaudet, the son of Reverend Thomas Hopkins Gallaudet.

In 1880, an international conference on education of the deaf in Milan, Italy, dealt a severe blow to the deaf community. This meeting of mostly European educators passed a resolution—158 to 6—claiming the superiority of oral education, which effectively led to a ban on the use of sign language in schools for the deaf. Five of the six votes against the resolution came from the American delegation, which included Edward Miner Gallaudet and James Denison, the only deaf attendee.[2] Over time, the oral method became the primary communication mode in many of the deaf schools in the United States. The number of deaf teachers and administrators at deaf schools dwindled, with most of the deaf teachers confined to the vocational classes.

In 1880, just before the Milan Congress, the American deaf community formed the National Association of the Deaf, an advocacy group to fight the threat of oralism and other matters such as discrimination. Its first meeting concluded with a resolution that stated "we have interests peculiar to ourselves which can be taken care of by ourselves."[3]

The oppression of sign language spilled over into oppression of deaf people in general, especially in employment opportunities and access to services readily available to the general population. For many years, deaf people were denied government and corporate jobs, driver's licenses, life and auto insurance, and access to easy communication with hearing people through ASL interpreters. They could not use the telephone

---

2. Douglas C. Baynton, Jack R. Gannon, and Jean Lindquist Bergey, *Through Deaf Eyes: A Photographic History of an American Community* (Washington, DC: Gallaudet University Press, 2007), 69.

3. Jack R. Gannon, *Deaf Heritage: A Narrative History of Deaf America* (Washington, DC: Gallaudet University Press, 2012), 62.

or understand dialogue in movies and television programs.[4] In the 1960s and 1970s, as more deaf people earned PhDs and professional degrees, things began to improve. Yet, something was missing—there had never been a deaf president of Gallaudet University, the pinnacle of deaf leadership. Furthermore, its board of trustees had never had a majority of deaf members.

When Jerry C. Lee resigned as president of Gallaudet in 1987, a rallying cry for a deaf president began to swell in the deaf community. Consequently, a wave of collective discontent began to gather into an unprecedented crescendo.

---

4. Gannon, *Deaf Heritage*, 157, 162, 320.

2

From Kendall Green to the Work World
and Back to My Alma Mater

I grew up in a deaf family, and looking back, I marvel at how my deaf parents managed to raise my sister, Sherry, and me in a world that was not equipped or ready to give deaf people the ability to control their own destiny. We lived in a three-room apartment in Mount Vernon, New York, where Sherry and I shared a bedroom. My dad was a machinist, and my mom was an office clerk, and we lived week to week on their paychecks. They invested everything they had in obtaining educations for Sherry and me. My father was involved in deaf community activities, primarily as a treasurer, and he used an old-fashioned adding machine to do those tasks. My parents and their friends were members of a deaf club in the community. Sylvan Riley, a Gallaudet graduate (class of 1918) lived a block from us. He had a clerical job but was a super intelligent guy, and my conversations with him opened many horizons for me. He always felt there was a way for deaf people to do better, and that put a fire in my belly to do more for the community. He said the way to do that was to control our destiny, but that required mobilization and telling the world that we weren't "broken"; we just needed an opportunity to prove ourselves. This led me to participate in student organizations and extracurricular activities at the New York School for the Deaf in White Plains. I also had deaf teachers and role models at the school (David Davidowitz, Bob Davila, and Taras Denis, all of whom were also Gallaudet alumni), who gave me the very same message that Mr. Riley did.

After I graduated from high school, I enrolled at Gallaudet in the fall of 1961. I had just turned sixteen and wasn't even shaving yet. During my preparatory year (the first year of Gallaudet's then five-year program), I had a deaf professor who was the first deaf Canadian to earn a doctorate. His name was Donald Kidd, and he was an anthropologist. I mention this because Dr. Kidd was one of only eleven deaf people in the world with an earned doctorate in 1961, a fact that is essential for understanding what was to come in the ensuing years at Gallaudet and for deaf education in general.

I had two other deaf mentors during my years at Gallaudet: Alan B. Crammatte, a professor in the Department of Business Administration who also was comptroller of the alumni office, and David Peikoff, executive director of the alumni office. Since I majored in accounting, I took a lot of courses from Crammatte, and I applied what I learned in his classes by working as a bookkeeper in the alumni office. Peikoff's wife, Polly, also worked in the office and was my mother away from home. She took care of me during my college years, nursing me with chicken soup whenever I had a cold.

Alan Crammatte and David Peikoff looked after and taught me well about many facets of leadership and the deaf community. They encouraged me to become active in various campus organizations, and I followed their advice. I was an editor of the class newspaper during my preparatory year, head freshman during my freshman year, secretary of the Student Body Government (SBG) during my sophomore year, and business manager of the student newspaper, the *Buff and Blue*. During that era at Gallaudet, the class "heads" (freshman, sophomore, etc.) were elected by their respective classmates. I was the male head freshman, and there was a female head freshman as well. We were the communication "glue" for the campus. One of our main responsibilities was to distribute the mail to classmates from the campus post office. Also, if any urgent messages needed to be delivered, we would do it at the same time we brought the mail. It was an effective means of "spreading the word" in addition to bulletin board postings at strategic campus locations. Obviously, due to our being deaf, loudspeakers were not useful, so face-to-face communication or announcements in the cafeteria were our means of communicating to the campus at large. During my senior year, I edited the yearbook, the *Tower Clock*. I also held several offices of the Kappa Gamma Fraternity. All these extracurricular activities, coupled with working under Peikoff and Crammatte, gave me the foundation for what was to happen in the years to come in the community and at Gallaudet.

After graduating from Gallaudet in 1966, I moved to Connecticut, where I started my career as a computer programmer for the Connecticut General Life Insurance Company, now known as CIGNA. After two years, at the urging of one of my Gallaudet classmates, I applied for and got a job at IBM as a systems programmer and moved to Saugerties, New York, a small hamlet between New York City and Albany. IBM had a large facility ten miles south in Kingston, New York. These were the early days of computer technology, and it was a fun job. I worked with a team of hardware and software engineers to put together a hardware/software package that IBM offered to airlines, banks, and insurance companies.

When my wife and I had two children (Jeff and Deb) who were deaf, we realized that there weren't any good programs for educating deaf children where we lived, so I requested and got a transfer to an IBM facility in the metropolitan New York City area. Our children could then attend the Lexington School for the Deaf in Queens. My job with IBM in New York City was the dream assignment of a lifetime. I was part of a team that went into hospitals, banks, insurance companies, newspapers, and credit card companies to analyze their workflows and design systems to computerize their day-to-day functions.

While living on Staten Island, Judy and I had a third deaf child (Seth), and I began to dabble in community activism, getting involved with deaf advocacy organizations in New York City and New York State. Captioning for TV programs was a buzzword for activism in those days because television was not accessible to me, my family, and the entire deaf community. The idea of doing something that made a difference for deaf people was a shot of adrenaline for me. During the day, I did that at IBM; at night, I did that for the family and the community. In subsequent years, I became very involved in local, state, and national deaf organizations that focused on advocacy issues. Initially, I concentrated on closed captioning, and later, I got involved in telecommunications (TTYs and eventually, video relay service).

I crossed paths with Gallaudet once again in 1978 when Edward C. Merrill, the president of the college, asked me to serve on the board of fellows, an advisory board to the board of trustees. The fellows met once or twice a year on campus and focused on single-subject matters. I saw this as an opportunity to repay Gallaudet for the foundation it helped me build professionally and personally, so I gladly accepted.

My work on the board of fellows also allowed me to learn more about Gallaudet. In 1979, our eldest son, Jeff, appeared as the title character in the CBS-TV movie *And Your Name Is Jonah*. That movie was a classic portrayal of a deaf child who was misdiagnosed as mentally disabled. Sally Struthers of *All in the Family* fame played his mother in the movie. Dr. Merrill and his wife, Frances, were fond of Jeff because of that movie role and invited us for a visit to House One (the president's home on campus). The Merrills saw Jeff as a role model for other deaf children in the country and wanted to recognize him for that. Dr. Merrill had a way of elevating deaf people of all ages to show the world that no limits should be imposed on deaf people, and Jeff was one of them. They entertained Jeff with tales of ghosts at House One. With my service on the board of fellows and this visit, I got the opportunity to better know Dr. Merrill. Subsequently, through that connection, one thing led to another—culminating in my nomination and appointment to the Gallaudet University Board of Trustees in 1981, at the age of thirty-six.

3

Setting the Presidential
Precedent: 1864–1983

The history of Gallaudet College begins in 1857, when Amos Kendall, a former postmaster general, donated property in northeast Washington, DC, for a school for orphaned deaf children that would be funded by the federal government. He then hired Edward Miner Gallaudet, a young teacher, to be the superintendent.[5] Though he was only twenty years old, Gallaudet accepted Kendall's offer with the hope that eventually he could convince Congress to establish a college for deaf students. He succeeded in 1864 when the National Deaf-Mute College (now Gallaudet University) was established by an act of Congress with President Abraham Lincoln's support and signature.

Edward Miner Gallaudet became the first president of the National Deaf-Mute College. Amos Kendall, who had donated ninety-nine acres for the school, became the first chair of the board of trustees. At that time, the board consisted of community leaders in Washington, DC, and members of Congress. (Today, deaf community leaders also serve on the board.) Kendall served as chair until his death in 1869. Earlier in that same year, he delivered the commencement address to the first graduating class. The original elementary school became part of the college, and it remains so to this day. Very few places in the United States today have a K–12 program and a university managed by the same executive team.

During Edward Miner Gallaudet's tenure, the institution grew from twelve to one hundred students, and he was

---

5. Edward Miner Gallaudet was the son of Thomas Hopkins Gallaudet of Hartford, Connecticut, the cofounder of the first permanent school for deaf children in the United States.

successful at retaining and even increasing funding from Congress. He retired in 1910 after serving the institution for fifty-three years, with forty-six years as its president.

Percival Hall became the second president of the college. He was a graduate of Harvard and Gallaudet's Normal School (the teacher-training graduate department). He had taught math at the college, been the head of the Normal School, and was Edward Miner Gallaudet's secretary. During his tenure, enrollment grew, the curriculum expanded, and the college's reputation spread, despite the political and economic upheavals of two world wars and the Great Depression. Gallaudet graduates became teachers of the deaf, professionals in many different fields, and leaders in their respective communities.

Dr. Hall retired in 1945 and was succeeded by Leonard M. Elstad, who was then superintendent of the Minnesota School for the Deaf. Like Hall, Elstad was a graduate of the Gallaudet Normal School. He had devoted his career to the education of deaf students, first as a Gallaudet faculty member and then as an administrator at various schools. Dr. Elstad was quick to note after his arrival that Gallaudet's facilities and programs needed improvement and that the college also needed to be accredited. He hired George Detmold, an English professor and assistant dean of the College of Arts and Sciences at Cornell University, to revamp the curriculum, hire new faculty, and work toward gaining accreditation. Elstad oversaw the construction of new buildings and the recruitment of more students, and, in 1957, their efforts were rewarded by receiving accreditation from the Middle States Association.

The college continued to grow in the 1960s; the student body swelled from some three hundred students to close to one thousand. I had the fortune of being a student at Gallaudet during Dr. Elstad's tenure. He was a charming man, had a unique signing style, and wrote wonderful letters. I recall getting a letter from him while I was a student. The letter arrived later than it should have, something Elstad had anticipated because he ended the letter with, "if it comes too late to be useful, just use the wastebasket." I think this pretty well sums up the spunky personality of this man who always made the time to greet everyone he saw on campus. During every new student orientation, he gave his "I Am Third" speech. I was a group leader during orientation for most of my student years, and I never missed his talk. To this day, I use his message as a mantra for many of my activities. It is a simple one—"God is first, everyone else is second, and myself, I am third." It reflects Dr. Elstad's unselfishness—he always shared credit with everyone and never forgot to send a thank you letter when it counted the most.

Dr. Elstad announced his retirement in early 1969, and the board (then a small group) embarked on a search that resulted in the hiring of Dr. Edward C. Merrill Jr., who was then the dean of the College of Education at the University of Tennessee. The method of selecting Merrill was not unusual; no formal search for Gallaudet's presidents had ever been done. In fact, very little is documented in the Gallaudet Archives or published about the functions of the board of trustees during Gallaudet's, Hall's, and Elstad's tenures. And it's worth mentioning that only two histories of the college have been published—the first in 1964, written by Albert Atwood,[6] chair of the board from 1946 to 1968, in celebration of the centennial of Gallaudet; and the second in 2014, written by David F. Armstrong, a former professor and budget director of the university, in celebration of the 150th anniversary of the founding of Gallaudet.[7]

Merrill's appointment was unusual in one way—he was the first Gallaudet president who did not have any experience in educating deaf students. However, once he arrived on campus,

---

6. Albert W. Atwood, *Gallaudet College, Its First One Hundred Years* (Lancaster, PA: Intelligencer Printing Company, 1964).

7. David F. Armstrong, *The History of Gallaudet University: 150 Years of a Deaf American Institution* (Washington, DC: Gallaudet University Press, 2014).

he learned sign language, and he and his wife, Frances, made the campus a home away from home for the students. He was a very popular president. In 1970, Gallaudet had approximately one thousand students, and Kendall School still served as the elementary school for deaf students in the Washington, DC, area. Despite the increase in campus facilities during Elstad's term, only about 50 percent of Gallaudet's ninety-nine-acre campus was developed. With increased funding from Congress for construction, Merrill oversaw the building of new residence halls, a new dining hall, a new library, a field house, the Kendall Demonstration Elementary School, and the Model Secondary School for the Deaf (MSSD). Merrill recognized that it was essential to invest in the younger generation of deaf students, so they could, in turn, enter Gallaudet when they got older—a very productive pipeline of students.

Late in Merrill's term, Gallaudet faced a new challenge. The population of college-age deaf students had increased dramatically due to the rubella epidemic of the mid-1960s. Approximately eight thousand children were born deaf during the outbreak because their mothers had contracted rubella in the first trimester of pregnancy. Dr. Merrill warned the board of trustees about this "rubella bulge," and Gallaudet began to gear up to accommodate these students. Instead of building new facilities for what we believed would be a temporary increase in students, we acquired the campus of the former Marjorie Webster Junior College in northwest Washington, DC, a very attractive area of town. The federal government owned the property and was not using it, so it was transferred to Gallaudet along with funds for renovations.

The Northwest Campus became the home of the preparatory program. We refurbished the buildings and hired faculty and staff to educate the incoming students. After completing their core courses, the students then transferred to the main campus to continue their education. Gallaudet eventually eliminated the preparatory program, but I feel good about being part of the effort in taking care of the rubella bulge. This was an astute effort by Gallaudet to meet the needs of deaf students who otherwise would have missed out on a college education for lack of space and facilities. Gallaudet eventually sold the property in the early 1990s after the "bulge" passed.

Another one of the hallmarks of Merrill's administration was the appointment of deaf people to administrative positions. The number of deaf managers, directors, and deans increased dramatically in the 1970s and early 1980s. Looking back (with the benefit of time), Dr. Merrill had a vision of Gallaudet's ultimate mission that remains to this day. Gallaudet evolved into a "cradle-to-grave" educational institution, serving children at Kendall School, high school students at MSSD, college students, graduate students, and adults in the community. He started to pave the way for deaf people to control their destiny by empowering them to enhance their community and professional credentials.

4

My Initial Years on the Board of Trustees (1981–1986)

To help readers appreciate the sequence of events that occurred at Gallaudet in 1988, I offer the following explanation of the workings of a university board of trustees. The key function of any board is to make policy for the university, not manage the university. The university's CEO or president manages the day-to-day issues of a university. After all, presidents are paid to do their job, while boards are usually composed of unpaid volunteers who donate their time and resources to the university. Some universities reimburse board members for travel; some don't. Most universities expect all their board members to contribute money annually. This 100 percent participation is what most donors (such as foundations or corporations) look for—it is a sign of any board's level of commitment. In any event, "the legal expectations of the duties of care, loyalty, and obedience are the essentials of board responsibility."[8]

The board president (or chair) is the point of contact when the university president needs to communicate matters that warrant the board's attention. It is usually up to the chair to decide whether to inform the other board members. The chair is an unpaid position, even though he or she is expected to be available for consultation with the president at any given time. Of course, any board member can talk to the president, but this needs to be kept to a minimum. It would tax the president's time and resources to be in touch with every member of the

8. Rick Legon, "The 10 Habits of Highly Effective Boards," *Trusteeship* (March/April 2014), accessed February 2, 2020, https://agb.org/trusteeship-issue/the-10-habits-of-highly-effective-boards-march-april-2014/.

board at all times. Of course, this does not preclude the president from being able to touch base with any board member, or vice versa. Using a typical employer-employee relationship, the president reports to the board through the board chair.

Many people believe that the primary function of any board of trustees is to hire or fire the president. I view this as a simplistic explanation, even though this is one of the key functions of any board. Board meetings vary in frequency among universities, but most meet three to four times a year. At the community college level, meetings are usually more frequent.

People often ask me how one gets appointed to a board. Again, this varies among universities. Some university boards, like Gallaudet's, are "self-perpetuating," meaning that the board itself screens and appoints members. In other situations, especially in state universities, elected officials, such as the governor, appoint members to such boards. In certain parts of the country, the public elects board members. The Gallaudet board has a provision where there are three congressional members (two from the House and one from the Senate). In addition, the Gallaudet University Alumni Association nominates one member.

What happens at a board meeting, and how does the board decide what to act on? While I was on the Gallaudet board, the process was as follows: Prior to a board meeting, the president works with senior staff in putting together an agenda. The president and board chair then go over it, either in person or over the phone, usually a few weeks before the meeting. Some agenda items are covered annually, such as budget approvals and tenure recommendations. Other items are done from time to time, such as approving the bylaws of the faculty and approving personnel decisions, such as salary adjustments. The remainder of the agenda usually consists of reports from the university's faculty and staff. Students do have the opportunity to report to the board as appropriate.

Gallaudet's board meetings take two to three days (some other boards meet only for a few hours because they meet more frequently). The timing and frequency, while arbitrary, do not take away the need to meet more frequently. This is done through special meetings, which can take place anytime with a specified agenda. The first day or day-and-a-half is usually spent in committees. The board bylaws define the committees, which usually cover the span of functions needed to run the university—academics, finances, investments, student life, and other things. The committee chair designated by the board and the senior official of the university designated by the president work out committee agendas.

After the committee meetings are finished, the full board convenes. The committee chairs report to the full board and ask for approval of those agenda items that require approval. The chairs may opt to comment on some items that were "reported" but did not require approval. The staff in attendance at such meetings can be called on to explain or amplify some agenda items before an action takes place. Some agenda items, such as honorary degrees or major policy decisions, are done at the full board level without going through board committees.

Time is usually set aside for "executive sessions," where personnel decisions and matters of a sensitive nature are covered. In those sessions, staff members are usually asked to leave, with only the president remaining. In matters where discussions about the president take place, such as compensation or evaluation, the president is also asked to leave. The president can opt to use this session as an opportunity to get the board's feedback on some pending decisions. Some boards, especially state university boards, have sunshine laws that define the scope of what members can discuss in executive sessions; at Gallaudet, the chair determines what matters can be discussed openly and what cannot.

Since Gallaudet's board is self-perpetuating, it has a committee on trustees, which is charged with the development of board members, from screening to interviewing prospective members. It also handles matters that affect the board, such as board conduct and board development. Up until 1988, Gallaudet's board members did not have term limits. After Deaf President Now (DPN), the board imposed limits of not more than four consecutive three-year terms. Those members who were on the board in 1988 were grandfathered in. I was the last pre-1988 board member when I stepped down after twenty years of service in 2001.

Gallaudet is in an unusual category. While it receives the bulk of its funding from the federal government, it is still a private university. The United States Department of Education has a liaison who works with Gallaudet. Congress annually receives recommendations from the Department of Education and receives testimony from the president of Gallaudet before it decides on the university's annual appropriation. Congress can choose to exceed or reduce the Department of Education's budgetary recommendation. Over the years, several congressional acts have defined the legal and statutory relationship between the US government and Gallaudet. The bottom line here is that the government extends to the Gallaudet board the responsibility for overseeing the university, as is spelled out in the Education of the Deaf Act of 1986, which states, "Gallaudet University is a federally chartered, private, nonprofit educational institution providing elementary, secondary, undergraduate, and continuing education programs for persons who are deaf."[9]

The most significant task of any board is to appoint a new president when the current president steps down or separates from the university, which usually results in a search process to replace the president. The search function is usually delegated to a search committee charged with the task of interviewing candidates, whittling down the pool, and recommending

---

9. Education of the Deaf Act of 1986, S. 1874, 99th Cong. (1986). https://www.govtrack.us/congress/bills/99/s1874.

finalists to the board. This particular function varies from one university to another. After the board has had the opportunity to interview the finalists, it then goes on to select the president, who then serves "at the pleasure of the board." The search process can take anywhere from several months to close to a year, and it is a major decision for any university.

I joined the board in 1981, and during my twenty years on the board, I had the opportunity to serve with five presidents at Gallaudet. I went through two major search processes as a board member, chairing one of them myself; this will be detailed further in this historical narrative. Of the five presidents, one retired and three resigned from the university, along with one incumbent.

In May of 1982, in an executive session of the board, Chair George Muth advised the board that Dr. Merrill had submitted his letter of resignation, which indicated his intention to leave Gallaudet in September 1983. The board members discussed the transition to the new president and agreed to plan the search for the fifth president at a later meeting. The board accepted Merrill's resignation with sincere regret and gave him a standing ovation in the boardroom.

Shortly after submitting his letter of resignation, Dr. Merrill composed a letter to George Muth to which he attached a paper on "Challenges Facing the Fifth President of Gallaudet College." He also drafted another paper titled "The Feasibility of a Deaf Person as President of Gallaudet College," but asked Muth to allow him to withhold the latter document.

In his letter to Muth, Merrill outlined the need for Gallaudet to have a deaf president, although he felt the justification was moot. Interestingly, he wrote that "the evidence on [sic] ability of deaf persons as administrators is already in and there is little more to say. A deaf person who is qualified has every right to hold the position and can reasonably be expected to do as well as a hearing person. Deafness, therefore, is no basis for questioning a qualified candidate, nor is it a basis which unduly recommends him." He also went on to say,

Although I have no further comment on the feasibility of a deaf person as president, I should like to bring to your attention the fact that deafness would be an asset to an individual serving as the fifth president of Gallaudet College in at least three ways: first, a deaf person serving as president would be seen as representative of the mission of the institution. He could speak both for deaf people and the College and would automatically have a level of credibility which could hardly be attained by a hearing person. Second, I think that a deaf person serving as president would be quite attractive to students who may aspire to attend Gallaudet College. Not only would students identify with him and have great confidence in his administration, but he would obviously be able to communicate quite clearly with them. Finally, a deaf president, even though he were not an alumnus of the institution, would obviously be a symbol of the success of education of deaf persons in this nation. After 118 years of educational effort, it would be timely, indeed, if a deaf person could assume the presidency of an institution of higher learning.

Looking back, even though I was not a member of the search committee to find Dr. Merrill's successor, I doubt this paper would have made an impact. Had it been made available to the board or even the public, it would have backfired. The board at that time was far from being ready to accept the fact that a deaf person could assume the presidency. The paper would have strengthened the board's resolve for a hearing person, viewing this as pushing them too hard in the direction of a deaf president. The bottom line is that the board members were not mentally ready because they did not understand nor appreciate the fact that deafness, per se, was an important factor, but not the only qualifying factor. Nor did they realize that this was why deaf people needed places like Gallaudet to make the "glass ceiling" more pliable, if not ready to be broken. Gallaudet was one of the only places in the country where a pool of proven deaf executives was in place and able to run the institution. Today, boards are more transparent, inclusive, and consultative compared to those in the 1980s.

The Feasibility of a Deaf Person as President
of Gallaudet College: An Unpublished Paper
by Dr. Edward C. Merrill Jr.

To this day, I cannot remember how I got my hands on
this particular paper (the only one that is not public).
I uncovered it while going through my papers in preparation for writing this book. This document does not exist
in the Gallaudet Archives, but I will donate it after this
book's publication.

Dr. Edward C. Merrill wrote this paper in July 1982,
after he had announced his retirement. In it, he clearly
lays out his intentions and thoughts. He personally
believed that the time was right for a deaf president after his tenure. I suspect he felt that the board of trustees was not ready to consider a deaf person, so instead,
he sent them a companion document that was not as
forceful as this unpublished document. With the benefit
of hindsight, I think Merrill made the right decision in
not sharing the unpublished document with the board,
which was starting the search for his replacement. Even
in 1987, when the board again was searching for a new
president, it would not have sat well with the board for
reasons already explained. The complete document can
be found at the end of this book.

Merrill's letter was like the battering ram used in medieval
warfare, trying to break down the gates of a castle. This gate
is akin to the glass ceiling that deaf people experienced for so
long and represented the board's mindset at that time. It was
thrust upon the deaf members of the board to then chip away
and soften the hardness of the glass ceiling.

The executive committee of the board met in August 1982 to discuss and start the search for Merrill's replacement. At that time, it was determined that the presidential search committee (PSC) would be composed of six trustees and that plans for the search would be provided to the public in September. The board eventually realized that the search needed to be more inclusive. As a result, the planned September announcement was shifted to take place after the October board meeting. In addition to the six trustees, the PSC consisted of three faculty representatives (two from the college and one from precollege programs), one staff representative, one alumni representative, and the president of the SBG. The board then charged the PSC to provide no less than two and no more than four finalists by March 1983.

I had been on the board a bit less than two years, so this was my first experience witnessing a search process at a university. As a newcomer, I was unaware of the politics starting to evolve on the board. I gradually learned that the board was divided into two camps, one composed of die-hard aging gentlemen, mostly businessmen from the Washington area, and the other composed of people who had joined the board several years before me. The older contingent included the board chair, George Muth, who was a well-known businessman in DC. He had served on the board for quite a number of years. The vice chair was Bradshaw Mintener, a Washington attorney who had helped launch the presidential campaigns of Dwight Eisenhower and Hubert Humphrey and who had served as assistant secretary of Health, Education and Welfare during the Eisenhower administration. He could be cantankerous, but he had a soft spot in his heart for Gallaudet. He was an interesting fellow to chat with.

Both Muth and Mintener were well into their seventies, and their advanced age was showing, but I was polite and slowly learned my way around the board. The other elderly gentlemen were Wilson Grabill, a Gallaudet alum who worked for the Census Bureau, and Frank B. Sullivan, then grand president of the National Fraternal Society of the Deaf. Frank ("Sully," as we all knew him) served with me on the board for some time until he stepped down in the 1990s. I replaced another deaf man, Ned Wheeler of Utah, who was a well-known leader in the community and wanted to "rest a bit." Since the 1950s, the deaf members of the board revolved around three to four deaf members. Boyce Williams (a Gallaudet alum for whom the current boardroom is named) was the first deaf board member elected in the 1950s.

The newer members of the board included Jane Bassett Spilman, part of the Bassett Furniture family empire, and Dr. Phil Sprinkle, an otolaryngologist from West Virginia. Dr. Sprinkle would prove to be a key member—he was a primary mover in restructuring the board as well as streamlining our investments as part of our endowment. Alexander Patterson and Gustave Rathe had worked together at IBM in New York in the late 1940s. Alex also served as a senior vice president of General Telephone and Electronics (GTE) Corporation, one of the independent phone companies that flourished in the 1970s and 1980s, and he was a force behind the creation of "Telenet," one of the first email systems used by the deaf community. Gustave also served on the first advisory board that led to the establishment of the National Technical Institute for the Deaf (NTID) at the Rochester Institute of Technology in the 1960s. Dr. Jim Hicks, another otolaryngologist from the University of Alabama in Birmingham, was a long-standing member of the board, but he aligned with the newer members.

I was appointed by the board chair to serve on the committee on trustees, which is the nominating committee of the board, charged with recruiting new board members as well as nominating board officers. Mine was an unusual appointment for a relatively new board member as it was traditionally extended to senior members. However, I later learned it was all orchestrated to have sufficient numbers "on the other side" to prepare for the "palace coup" of the board that took place near the end of Dr. Merrill's tenure. I was chosen (unbeknownst to me) to be part of the "other side" to counter the "team" of Muth and Mintener.

At one particular meeting in 1983, when nominations were to take place for officers of the board, Phil Sprinkle approached me to discuss how the board needed to change in order to prepare for the time when Dr. Merrill retired. He explained that Gallaudet was ready for new approaches to strengthening its investments and infrastructure, and the board needed to be ready to take the leap with a new and fresh leader. He suggested that Muth and Mintener would not be ready for this leap. The script for that nominating meeting was carefully planned with members of the committee on trustees to nominate certain members to replace the "Old Guard." Honestly, I was simply naive and went with the flow. I made some motions to change the leadership by recommending Jane Bassett Spilman as chair and Jim Hicks as vice chair. Dr. Sprinkle was nominated as treasurer. These motions changed the entire leadership of the board. I was kind of nervous at this meeting. Dr. Merrill sat across from me, and he winked at me when I made some of those motions, which reassured me and indicated that Merrill understood what was best for Gallaudet.

After the committee meeting, we met together as a full board to formalize and ratify the various committee motions. It must have been awkward for Muth and Mintener to sit through a meeting where they were being voted out as officers against their wishes.

While all this was going on, the PSC, chaired by Alex Patterson, was carrying on its work. The committee hired a consultant to conduct a national search, which was the first major search of its kind in Gallaudet's history. The previous searches were not as comprehensive as this one. I was not on the PSC, but the remaining board members and I received periodic reports by mail about the search process, with updates at every board meeting. We knew that there were some deaf candidates and that all references were being checked with a fine-tooth comb.

Ultimately, the board selected Dr. Lloyd Johns, then the provost of California State University at Sacramento. I recall Dr. Johns flying in with his wife to meet the board. At first glance, I was impressed with the guy. He had a good handle on a wide range of issues, and I felt good about the selection at that time.

Less than a year later, in January of 1984, Dr. Johns resigned the presidency due to personal reasons, leaving a leadership vacuum at Gallaudet. The board looked at the administrators on campus and settled on Jerry C. Lee, who was the vice president for Administration and Finance. He was an insider, had a good relationship with the board, and knew Gallaudet very well, having been on campus for a number of years. The board asked Lee to serve as interim president, but because we were uncertain whether he would measure up to the job, we set up a management review committee, consisting of myself as the chair along with Oliver Carr, Henry Ashforth, and Rex Rainer. (Ashforth was in real estate in New York and Rainer was a vice president of Auburn University.). I felt this was another measure of confidence that Jane Spilman had in me. Carr was a major player in real estate in Washington during that time and was Lee's neighbor in Great Falls, Virginia.

At the beginning of Lee's term, the management committee met with him on a monthly basis, and eventually every other month. After a few months, we felt that he was doing a good job, and we recommended to the board that he become president—taking away the "interim" tag.

Gallaudet experienced several gains during Lee's presidency. He developed a good relationship with Congress and the Department of Education, and the federal appropriation increased annually, as did the percentage of funds from tuition. The increase in funds allowed Lee to invest in the athletic

The board of trustees in a formal photograph with President Jerry C. Lee prior to the ceremony of Gallaudet College being elevated to university status. First row, left to right: Dr. Harvey J. Corson, Eloise Thornberry, Dr. Philip Sprinkle, Dr. Frank B. Sullivan, President Jerry C. Lee, Chairman Jane Bassett Spilman, Alexander E. Patterson Jr., and Oliver T. Carr Jr. Second row, left to right: George Muth, Dr. James J. Hicks, Dr. Robert G. Sanderson, Charles T. Haskell, Gustave H. Rathe Jr., and Dr. Philip W. Bravin (the author).

program, especially the football team, which hadn't had a winning season in many years. Bob Westermann became the head coach, and his teams surprised everyone with a succession of winning seasons.

In a nutshell, Gallaudet was on a roll. Unusual as it may seem, President Lee had business, not academic, credentials at that time, but he had a vision that kept us moving. His greatest accomplishment was to secure university status for Gallaudet. In 1985, he and Jane Spilman explained to the board that in view of its expanding mission and academics, as well as its increase in doctoral programs, it would make sense for Gallaudet to move up another notch. The board enthusiastically supported the change. Dr. Lee then approached Senator Lowell Weicker Jr. (R-CT), about sponsoring a bill that would grant university status to the college. Congress passed the Education of the Deaf Act in 1986, which, in part, changed Gallaudet from a college to a university. We had a big celebratory and formal event in the Field House, where the rechristening took place with full academic regalia. It was a beautiful event and, looking back, the change in status made much sense—after all, Gallaudet, as I said earlier, is a complex institution and a mecca, and it deserved university status.

5

Laying the Foundation for the Search

Life went on smoothly after the celebration at Gallaudet until I received the phone call from Jane Spilman in August 1987. After that call, things went into motion for the search to replace Dr. Lee. This was my first time heading a PSC, but having witnessed the search for Dr. Johns and being on search committees for several nonprofit boards, I felt comfortable starting the process. A search is almost a full-time job for the chair, and I already had a full-time job at IBM and a family to raise at home. Several formalities had to be taken care of, but the priority was to announce Dr. Lee's resignation to the board and the campus community. Next, I had to select the members of the PSC, reveal the composition of the committee, and then inform the campus of the forthcoming special board meeting and search committee meeting.

One may ask how such a committee is composed. It is usually a matter to be decided by the board chair and the chair of the PSC. Jane and I had a discussion, and we agreed to have as much campus and stakeholder representation as possible. It was a tricky and complicated endeavor at best. I had to take the board majority into account. But I also wanted the majority of the committee to be composed of deaf and hard of hearing individuals, and I believed we had to take gender balance into account as well. After the faculty and staff gave me their selections, both of whom were hearing, it was not possible to achieve a deaf majority. As it turned out, we had six hearing people and five deaf people on the PSC with voting privileges, with Jane Bassett Spilman as an ex officio member, which meant she had voice but no voting privileges.[10] As chair, I had voice and voting privileges, but because the chair needs to be neutral, I could use my vote only to break a tie, if need be. With Jane, we had seven men and five women on the PSC.[11]

As expected, I received letters from the campus and the deaf community, asking to be represented on the committee. While the interest was commendable, a balance had to be struck between enough representation and the size of the committee. A larger committee would make things unwieldy and more prone to leaks. The final decision was between Jane and me, and we felt we had a good cross section of the campus and the community. People might think this was an arbitrary decision, not involving the rest of the board. Once we decided on the committee's composition, we sent a letter to the board and a memo to the campus community to inform them.

The PSC had three deaf board members on it: myself, Dr. Robert Sanderson from Utah, and Dr. Frank Sullivan from Maryland. The other committee members were Dr. Laurel Glass, who was hard of hearing, from California, and two hearing people—Alexander Patterson from Connecticut and Gustave Rathe from Virginia. The university administration representative was the provost, Dr. Catherine Ingold, another hearing person. Two deaf people, Dr. Nancy Kensicki, the alumni representative, and Timothy Rarus, the student representative, as well as the student body president, also served. Dr. H. Neil Reynolds was the faculty representative (he also chaired the faculty senate), and Denise Sullivan, the university's director of human resources, represented the staff.

---

10. For some groups, a participant can have both voice and voting privileges. Usually if you have a guest who is also a colleague, but not part of the group, we, as a courtesy, extend voice privileges, meaning that person can express any opinion but not be able to vote since they are not a member of the group.

11. The board chair has full authority to establish ad hoc committees, one of which is a search committee. And with the board's approval, it becomes legitimate until the committee achieves its ad hoc mission.

Incidentally, I had known Timothy Rarus for a long time. After graduating from Gallaudet in 1966, I worked for an insurance company in Hartford, Connecticut, and my wife and I lived in Canton, near Timothy's parents. Occasionally, we babysat for them, and we even changed Timothy's diapers!

Alexander Patterson and Gustave Rathe had been on the board for more than twenty years, most of it in their retirement years. They were cut from practically the same cloth; both started their careers after college with IBM in New York City. During World War II, Alexander served as a fighter pilot, and Gustave was a naval supply officer stationed in the Pacific. After the war, they worked for IBM as salesmen in the New York City headquarters. Alexander once related to me that Tom Watson Jr., then the CEO at IBM, hated to see someone sitting in the office. He said a vacant chair in the office meant someone was out there selling and working with IBM's customers. Gustave moved up the ranks and became an executive there, and Alexander moved on to work at GTE, one of the major phone companies in the 1980s.

Both men were connected to the Southwest when they retired, where they remained active. Alexander became interested in ancient rock art, and Gustave took courses at St. John's College in Santa Fe, and they each wrote a book. Alexander wrote *A Field Guide to Rock Art Symbols of the Greater Southwest*, which was the first book of its kind when it was published in 1992. I recall him telling me he took pains not to identify the specific locations of the symbols for fear they would be defaced or destroyed by others in the years to come. Gustave wrote *The Wreck of the Barque Stefano Off the North West Cape of Australia in 1875*, which also was published in 1992. While the title sounded cryptic and not significant, it documented the adventures of his maternal grandfather, Captain Miho Baccich of Dubrovnik, Croatia, who had been shipwrecked off the coast of Australia in 1875. Gustave was also an avid sailor, an accomplished watercolorist, and an aficionado of ornithological art and bird decoys.

Being an IBM-er myself at the time of the search, Gustave, Alexander, and I had a common bond, which lasted for many years. I consider them both to be among my mentors. Sitting at a dinner table with them was always a treat; they never lacked a story that generated a laugh. In the boardroom, they were both involved and perceptive. Gallaudet is a better place today, mainly due to the contributions of them both on the board. I miss them very much.

Dr. Frank Sullivan and Dr. Robert Sanderson were members of Gallaudet's class of 1941. They served on the board with me before, during, and after the DPN movement. Frank came with an institutional memory and often helped navigate the board when it came to historical precedence or instances that sometimes had a bearing on our decisions.

He had been on the board for a number of years when I was appointed. Robert joined the board after I did, and the three of us became strong allies during the months leading up to DPN. They were twenty-five years my senior, and I looked up to them; they were always in full support of my role as chair of the PSC and counseled me during some difficult moments. Frank was grand president of the National Fraternal Society of the Deaf, an insurance company that provided services to the deaf population. Robert was an administrator in rehabilitation services for the deaf in Utah and had served as president of the National Association of the Deaf.

Dr. Laurel Glass joined the board in the mid-1980s. She was both an academic and a medical doctor, and she was hard of hearing. She made significant contributions while on the board's academic affairs committee by virtue of her background as a faculty member of the University of California at San Francisco and her grasp of traditional university policies, especially as they related to the faculty. At one time during her tenure, she advocated for divestment of tobacco stocks, which the board eventually adopted.

A California native, Laurel received an undergraduate degree from the University of California, Berkeley, a PhD in biology from Duke University, and a medical degree from the University of California, San Francisco. Much of her research was devoted to the impact of hearing loss on individuals, especially older people.

I had known Dr. H. Neil Reynolds, Denise Sullivan, Dr. Catherine Ingold, and Dr. Nancy Kensicki for some time. Dr. Kensicki was a year ahead of me at Gallaudet, and in those days, Gallaudet had a small student body of about 500–600 students. Practically everyone knew everyone. Reynolds, Sullivan, and Ingold often attended board meetings because of their positions.

This was the agenda for the PSC's first meeting. Courtesy of the author's personal files.

Jane Spilman sent a memo to the board members to inform them that there would be a "special" meeting on campus
on September 15. This meeting would be in addition to the
"regular" meeting scheduled for October. She included a list
of agenda items, so if other actionable items came up during
the meeting that were not part of the agenda, they couldn't be
discussed and would need to be referred to the executive committee. The executive committee had the authority to act on
items between regular board meetings with certain limitations.
Spilman also told the board that the first meeting of the PSC
would take place that weekend.

The agenda for the meeting was as follows:
• Discussion of Dr. Jerry Lee's resignation
• Presentation of the plans for the search
• Composition of the search committee
• Preparation of a draft of the announcement to the
  campus
• Approval of the statement of qualifications for the posi-
  tion of president
• Approval of the charge to the search committee
• Approval of the job announcement for the position of
  president
• Review of the interim university governance plan

I then started working on the charge with Lil Holt, knowing
more changes would be made at the meeting. The charge is an
important document because it lists what the board expects
from the PSC, and I thought it would be helpful for the board
to have something with which to start.

The meeting on September 15 was tenuous at best. During
the meeting, it became obvious that certain board members
were disturbed by the fact that President Lee was leaving Gallaudet to work for Jane Spilman's husband. Jane staunchly de-
fended this and told the board members she did not know any

details of the conversation on this topic between her husband and President Lee.[12]

We then discussed the composition of the PSC and the statement of qualifications for the new president. I believe this is a difficult task for any university board. Because of Gallaudet's unique mission, we also faced the dilemma of deciding whether to find the best person for Gallaudet or to find the best deaf person for the position. Some may ask why we couldn't find both qualities in the same person, but most of the board wanted to have a large pool of applicants, and this would not have been possible if we made deafness or fluency in sign language a requirement. Only three of us on the board were deaf—Bob Sanderson, Frank Sullivan, and myself—so we could push only so hard for this. Instead, we tempered the requirement to read "a proficiency in or the commitment to learn sign language," and the rest of the board approved this language.

As chair of the PSC and being deaf myself, I was torn internally. Privately, I wanted a deaf person for the job, but my position required me to create a pool of the best candidates out there for Gallaudet, whether they were deaf or hearing. Some in the deaf community may have disagreed with me on this, but I felt my responsibility was to do what was in the university's best interests, that is, to find the best person to become president.

The board completed the statement of qualifications and finalized the charge to the PSC. The members requested that the committee present no less than three candidates to the board. They also reviewed the job announcement. The announcement, along with the statement of qualifications, formed the basis for communicating to the public about the position. Additionally, we discussed where to place the ads for the position and agreed

---

12. Although I won't reveal any more details of the board members' comments, this should not take away from the wonderful relationship I had with Jane until then and going forward.

that the major newspapers and the deaf press would initially be used as the primary vehicles.

Contrary to common thought and belief, the mission of the search committee was to facilitate the search process, not select the next president. Because the PSC members represented various constituencies of the university, they were in the best position to interview and narrow down the pool of candidates to a manageable number. Once we had done that, the board of trustees would make the final decision on whom to appoint.

The next order of business was to decide who would govern the university when Dr. Lee left. Many presidential transitions tend to overlap a bit; however, we were in an unusual situation because he had given us a little over three months' notice to prepare for his exit. Instead of designating an interim president, as we had when Lee's predecessor resigned, we decided to set up a team, the Central Administration Management Team (CAMT for short). It was composed of four senior administrators: Catherine Ingold, the provost; Jim Barnes, the vice president of business and administration; Robert Davila (deaf), the vice president of precollege programs; and Merv Garretson (deaf), the special assistant to the president. Communication lines were set between the team and Jane Spilman for board matters. The CAMT would manage Gallaudet's day-to-day operations but not make major decisions or undertake new initiatives.

After the board meeting ended, the search committee met. Jane presented the full charge to the committee, which read as follows:

> The board of trustees requests that the presidential search committee adopt a single committee concept and it stresses that each member of the committee has an obligation to act in the best interest of Gallaudet University rather than as a representative of the constituency with which he or she may be identified. Similarly, degrees of confidentiality and openness are expected of the committee.

The presidential search committee is responsible for identifying and developing a diverse pool of qualified candidates. This is the most critical phase of the search process. While formal recruiting activities associated with the search such as advertising in appropriate journals, sending notices to relevant associations, and writing to knowledgeable people will be employed, it is suggested that the presidential search committee utilize informal approaches to identify persons who merit consideration for the position.

The board of trustees entrust the presidential search committee with the task of submitting the names of no less than three but no more than five candidates who meet the qualifications for the position of president to the full board by the 6th of December. The board will interview the candidates on the 16th and 17th of December and it anticipates formally announcing the name of the seventh president on Monday, December 21, 1987.

We then distributed the position announcement, and the committee had the opportunity to review it and ask questions. It was essential for all the committee members to be on the same page and understand the material that was shared.

I shared the following statement of qualifications with the rest of the committee. We were to use the list while screening candidates for the position. We didn't mean it to be a rigid document; any applicant with borderline qualifications tended to be screened in, rather than out. After all, no one person would strongly meet all the requirements, so we needed to have some flexibility.

Statement of Qualifications
- an earned doctorate degree;
- demonstrated or be judged capable of demonstrating a sensitive understanding of and commitment to the hearing impaired;
- proven management skills;
- the capacity to be an effective spokesperson for the university;

- fundraising skills, including the ability to work effectively with Congress, federal agencies, foundations, corporate officers, and with persons of substance;
- the ability to maintain rapport with faculty, staff, students, alumni, and other constituencies of the university;
- a management style that emphasizes consultation and delegation;
- an effective communicator including writing and public speaking;
- a proficiency in or the commitment to learn sign language; and
- a certain visionary quality regarding the mission of Gallaudet University.

After reviewing the list of qualifications, we discussed the approximate timetable for the search. We based it on a best-case scenario that assumed everything would go perfectly. The board members had projected that they would announce their decision on December 21 to minimize the time between Dr. Lee's exit and the installation of the new president. The PSC felt that the cutoff date of October 26 for the submission of applications was too short and voted to extend the date to November 26, which pushed the final selection date from December to February. Between December and February, the CAMT would manage the campus.

To facilitate the review of applications, the committee set up a screening subcommittee composed of the campus representatives (Ingold, Reynolds, Kensicki, and Rarus). The screening was scheduled for late November after the cutoff date for applications.

Finally, we laid the ground rules for the committee. I told the committee that confidentiality was of the utmost importance, and leaks would not be tolerated. If anyone leaked confidential information, they would be immediately removed from the committee. The high-profile nature of this search necessitated that action, especially given the deaf community's heightened expectations.

9-15-87

GALLAUDET **G** UNIVERSITY

PRESIDENTIAL SEARCH COMMITTEE

PRESIDENT

KENDALL GREEN
800 FLORIDA AVENUE, N.E.
WASHINGTON, D.C. 20002

The Presidential Search Committee of Gallaudet University invites nominations and applications for the position of president. The president is the Chief Executive Officer of the institution and is responsible to the Board of Trustees.

Gallaudet University is a private, liberal arts institution incorporated in 1864 by an act of Congress, and is the world's greatest resource on deafness. The University responds to several federal laws which authorize and support its programs and services; however, it is not a federal agency and the Board of Trustees is solely responsible for the institution.

The Committee seeks candidates who by their record have demonstrated the ability to lead an institution of Gallaudet's unique character and composition and who will be challenged by the opportunity to be president at a university committed to leadership in educational programs and services for hearing impaired persons.

The candidate should have an earned doctorate and should present evidence of broad successful administrative leadership and proven management effectiveness in education, industry, or other large organizations; demonstrated skills to obtain, manage, and allocate financial resources; the ability to work effectively with national and international constituencies; and the experience and personal qualities necessary for the continued development of an institution with a specialized and critically important mission.

Broad and deep knowledge of deafness and the variety of issues important to the higher education of hearing impaired persons is necessary. Sensitivity to the issues significant to individuals with disabilities and demonstrated success in dealing with those concerns may be an acceptable alternate. Proficiency in or the willingness to learn sign language is mandatory. Applications and nominations from hearing impaired persons are encouraged.

Candidates should send a letter of application, current resume and three current references. Applications and supporting papers must be postmarked by the filing deadline, November 26, 1987, and should be sent to:

Mr. Philip W. Bravin, Chair
Presidential Search Committee
Gallaudet University
Post Office Box 2366
800 Florida Avenue, N.E.
Washington, D. C. 20002

A detailed description of the University is available upon request.

Gallaudet University is an Equal Opportunity, Affirmative Action Employer

This was an information sheet inviting nominations and applications for the position of president of Gallaudet University. Note the provision regarding sign language. Courtesy of the author's personal files.

The committee asked for both nominations and applications. If a person or an organization nominated someone, Lil Holt sent a letter in my name to that person, informing them of their nomination and that they were welcome to apply for the position. All the nominations, whether they came from an individual or a group, received the same treatment. Some applications came to the committee without a nomination. Some nominations, especially those from a group, were indicative of the group's agenda for the position. This was particularly true for groups that were advocating for a deaf president. A group that advocated for female executives nominated a female candidate, and some groups nominated several candidates.

From that point on, Lil and I kept in touch every now and then via TTY or mail. We didn't have email back then, but I was at her beck and call twenty-four hours a day, seven days a week for the duration of the search. Lil was also my conduit to Jane, and I usually communicated with her whenever the need arose. Since I saw Jane relatively often during the process, we had many opportunities to meet and chat about the process.

The search created a lot of attention and commotion on campus, especially over the possibility of Gallaudet having its first deaf president. Rumor after rumor (some of which were not necessarily factual) circulated, and I tried my best to be oblivious to them by sheltering myself back home in New York. Lil provided me all the necessary information to move on with the search. I also tried my best not to be biased by all the attention related to the search in the deaf community. Any response to such commotions would create more commotions and rumors. Dealing with facts and information on a "need-to-know" basis was the order of the day. Looking back, that served us well.

6

Starting the Engines: The Search Begins

The campus learned about the September board meeting in an article published in *On the Green*, the campus newsletter for faculty and staff. The board members agreed we could do the search without a consultant, so we put the wheels in motion accordingly. We started placing ads in national newspapers—the *New York Times*, the *Chronicle of Higher Education*, among others—and in as many deaf publications as we could reach.

The applications started to roll in. Most of the applications were in the form of a resume/curriculum vitae and a cover letter. Personally, I was more interested in the cover letter and seeing how it "rhymed" with the rest of the documentation. But as chair, I remained steadfastly neutral. I knew all eyes were on the committee, especially me as the chair. Every word I uttered was subject to analysis, speculation, and reading between the lines; over time, I began to develop a style that made it difficult for people to figure where I was coming from.

When asked how the search was going, I would usually respond by saying, "we are moving along and we have some milestones. It has been going smoothly as any search would." When the question came up about deaf candidates, the stock answer would be "our mission is to find the best person for Gallaudet, deaf or hearing. Of course, deaf people are welcome and encouraged to apply." People would ask why we limited the committee to eleven people, and the answer was "we did not want a big committee so as to make things unwieldy. We did not want a small committee that would leave out some stakeholders. While not perfect, we tried to strike a balance in this regard, not too big, not too small, and as inclusive as possible." Of course, some people wanted a more definitive answer, but

I had to stick to the "party line" and, above all, be consistent. If I gave a different answer for the same question down the road, it would come back to haunt me, and I would have to explain that away. I believe I was as consistent as I could be.

Here are some examples of my responses during interviews:

—*I was honored to be asked, [as chair] and will serve with pleasure.*

—*The setting and the environment in Vermont were perfect for sitting down and thinking about whether I could accept this assignment . . . and, after thinking, I knew it was a challenge that I wanted to take on, and one I felt confident that I could handle well.*

—*The individual selected will face several immediate challenges along with the job: the rapidly changing federal climate; the rapidly changing mix of students at Gallaudet; and the struggle to maintain Gallaudet traditions.*

—*I am confident that the search process will uncover a number of highly qualified deaf individuals.*

—*There is a pool of qualified hearing and deaf candidates out there. The deaf community has also developed a pool of excellent candidates. The final result should be the best possible person to serve as the seventh president of Gallaudet University.*

My standing in the community also created some interesting scenarios. For example, when I was selected chair of the search committee, I was serving as secretary of the National Association of the Deaf (NAD). By virtue of being secretary of the organization, I also served on the executive board of the NAD. During NAD board meetings, because the NAD had a vested interest in the presidency of Gallaudet, it advocated for a deaf president. Every time the Gallaudet search process came on the agenda during board meetings, I recused myself and left the room while the deliberations took place. Any official actions taken as a result of such deliberations were stated and made before I went back into the room. As secretary, I had to handle the minutes of such board meetings and have them approved at subsequent meetings. For the duration of the presidential search, however, I didn't see the minutes for that part of the meeting. It was a bit of a logistical situation until the search process ran its course.

Being a visible part of the deaf community, everywhere I went during the search process, people didn't refer to me as Phil Bravin; instead, I was "the person who is leading the search for Gallaudet's next president." I was constantly subjected to questions and comments from members of the community everywhere I went—social events, meetings, outings, sporting events, and so forth. I tried my best to insulate my children from the process and, at the same time, gave them talking points should people ask them questions about the search.

In addition to the search committee, I still had a full-time job to contend with. I was marketing programs administrator at IBM's US headquarters in White Plains, NY. I was responsible for a team that created marketing programs, initiatives, and materials for use by our sales force and customers in our branches across the country. This required working with our development and manufacturing teams across the country, understanding the products and services that were to be rolled out, and then developing the information to support the rollout. IBM had a very wide range of products. My team focused on the personal computer (or the Personal System/2, as it was known then officially).

At the beginning of the presidential search, I advised the management at IBM that my involvement would sometimes take me away from my job during the day, but I promised to work evenings and weekends when the situation warranted. In other words, my work at IBM would not be compromised.

IBM, as a matter of practice, encouraged its employees to perform community service, so this arrangement worked out perfectly for IBM and me, and I am eternally grateful for this. Gustave Rathe, who had retired from IBM, had standing with the executive management of the company, and he wrote a letter to the then-CEO, John Akers, advising him of my role in the search and asking the company to be considerate of my time requirements. As it turned out, IBM never questioned my time away from the office during the search. I also worked very hard to ensure that my duties were not compromised by the search.

As I mentioned earlier, my strong deaf roots added to my realization that Gallaudet would someday have a deaf president. At the same time, I had a duty to facilitate the process to pick the next leader of Gallaudet from a pool that consisted of deaf and hearing people. It truly was a personal dilemma, and I tried my best to rise above this inner struggle in order not to compromise the integrity of the search.

The board met in late October and went into executive session during the two-and-a-half-day meeting. During the executive session, Jane Spilman reported that the executive committee had been working with the CAMT and that the chair, Catherine Ingold, would be the spokesperson for the administration during the transition. The CAMT would meet monthly (more often if necessary) and would work with the board's executive committee when the situation warranted. The executive committee would have the discretion to decide whether or not to consult with the full board.

During the executive session, the committee on trustees of the board proposed that the board consider appointing Larry Speakes, president of the Merrill Lynch Foundation and President Reagan's former press secretary, to the board. The members authorized Jane Spilman and Dr. Jerry Lee to visit Larry Speakes and invite him to join the board. The bylaws stipulate that the board be limited to twenty-one members, including the three public members—one congressman from each party and a senator from the majority party. There was a vacancy on the board at the time, and Speakes seemed like the perfect fit. I then gave a progress report on the search without going into details about the applicants. I explained that applications were coming in slower than we would like, but we were monitoring the process. I passed out the revised statement of qualifications adopted by the committee for the board members to review. I also explained that a prescreening committee was being set up, using the statement of qualifications as a basis for screening. One member asked whether it was a requirement for the president to live in House One, the official residence of the president of Gallaudet. This issue came out of the blue, but later on, it became clear that the requirement for living on campus could be a deterrent to some candidates for various reasons. The board ultimately instructed the committee to make this requirement optional. Lastly, we discussed the revised timetable for the search.

The search committee met after the board meeting to discuss recruitment and the screening of the resumes, curricula vitae and cover letters that were coming in. Some committee members wondered if the pool of applicants was deep enough and whether we needed to step up recruitment. I indicated to the committee that we had the option of bringing in a search consultant, and I told them that the board had informally discussed this idea earlier in the day.

In early November, a memo went out to the campus outlining the status of the search at that point. It explained that the search committee had a plan for screening and interviewing candidates and for continuing to recruit to increase the pool of potential candidates; however, it did not mention that we were planning to retain a search firm. In addition, it said that screening would take place throughout November and that the search process was expected to conclude in the first quarter of 1988.

The screening subcommittee met on several occasions during the month of November. Its function was to quickly review the applications and group them into three piles based on how well the applicants met the qualifications. The first pile consisted of people to consider for interview, the second pile was for those whose qualifications required consensus of the full committee in order to be considered, and the third pile was for those who did not meet the qualifications. The screening subcommittee did not have final say on any of the piles; the full search committee would make the decision on who to interview at their meeting in early December. As always, Lil was on top of this and coordinated the logistics for that process.

At one of our early November meetings, Catherine Ingold, who headed the screening subcommittee, said that a preliminary assessment had determined we had sixteen viable deaf and hearing candidates out of a pool of approximately seventy-five applicants, and of those sixteen, about half were worth looking at further. After some discussion with Jane Spilman, Alexander Patterson, Gustave Rathe, and Frank Sullivan, we decided that the candidate pool was not large enough for a credible search, especially with respect to deaf candidates. I felt there were more deaf people out there who could be considered for the job, and maybe some just needed a "push." As the neutral chair of the search committee, I couldn't do the pushing, but a headhunter could. We considered reopening the search but ultimately decided it would be more effective to hire an external search firm. Jane said she would consult with the executive committee of the board for their approval.

The executive committee of the board gave its approval, and I immediately began efforts to locate a search firm. Since all the applications were due by November 26, we had a very short period of time to find a firm and recruit more applicants. Changing the November 26 date would send the wrong signal, like the current applicants were not good enough or the like and could have had the effect of some applicants withdrawing their applications. I had to be sure that the search firm was a good match for the university, the members of the search committee, and Jane. The key was whether the firm could quickly pick up the unique aspects of deafness and the culture of the deaf community.

I interviewed two firms in person on campus, and my gut told me they were not a good match for us. I then got a referral from Gustave Rathe for a search firm in, of all places, Nantucket, Massachusetts. Gus had a vacation home on Nantucket, and he had coincidentally met with one of the principals of the search firm. One of Gus's colleagues at IBM had recommended the firm because the trustees of St. Lawrence University had retained them for their successful presidential search. Through an interpreter, I called Nancy Archer-Martin, one of the principals of that firm, the Education Management Network. After she gave me more information, I checked some references and decided to fly out to Nantucket to interview her.

In an effort to see how Nancy would react to working with a deaf client, I decided to go up there without an ASL interpreter. Many people who have never dealt with deaf people before exhibit a level of discomfort when trying to communicate for the simple reason that our mode of communication is so different for those folks. Not us, though; we're used to different communication situations as deaf people. A cold turkey treatment like this would test Nancy's tolerance and acceptance up front. Search firms do not come cheap—they usually charge from half the salary of a president to a full year's salary as part of their fee, plus expenses—and we didn't have much time, so I had to be sure we were not risking the university's assets in this endeavor.

Off I went, flying out of LaGuardia to Boston and then changing to a puddle jumper to Nantucket. Landing in Nantucket was eerie; there was water all around and then suddenly the airport appeared. I walked into the terminal, a small building with gray shake shingles and looked around. A few minutes later, a woman appeared in the baggage claim area obviously looking for someone, and I figured it was Nancy. I said "Nancy?" She answered "yes," and we shook hands and went to her car.

For hearing people who have never dealt with a deaf person before, traveling in a car with a deaf passenger is the ultimate in discomfort. First of all, the driver can't talk looking straight ahead on the road because it is almost impossible to lipread someone sideways. I consider myself a pretty good lipreader, but lipreading sideways takes away almost all accuracy and guesswork. So a driver has to look at my face and utter whatever they want to say. Nancy caught onto this quickly; she looked at me and asked "coffee?" I said "yes," and she stopped at a cafe on the way to her office.

We arrived at her home, which also served as her office, clad in typical Nantucket gray siding. Nancy made a sincere effort to converse with me via a variety of means—we wrote back and forth, she talked and tried to understand my deaf speech, and I lipread some. After an hour, I became more comfortable with her and how she approached things. I laid everything on the table and did all I could to detail our progress with the search. I started off the conversation by explaining what we had done, to date, on the search. While we felt we were doing pretty well, we just needed help on enhancing the pool, especially with respect to deaf candidates.

Nancy really drilled me on our process—how we set up the search, who was on the committee, and how the board managed the whole thing. She wanted to be sure she wasn't coming in to do damage control, which, in the end, could reflect on the integrity of her firm. That I understood very well, and I was very honest with her, leaving no stone unturned. I also gave her a historical overview of Gallaudet, as well as Gallaudet's standing in the community. I was very aware that the cultural aspect of deafness was totally new to her, so I used the analogy of historically black colleges and women's colleges to help drive that point forward. Basically, while it was an introductory meeting, I was also under pressure to move the process forward. Had Nancy turned this down, I would have needed to find another firm and potentially delay the process.

We continued the conversation in a restaurant before Nancy took me back to the airport for my flight back to LaGuardia. I had the impression that she was willing to take up the challenge, and I felt very comfortable with her for two reasons. First, she seemed at ease in dealing with a deaf person and was adaptable in her approach to conversation and in eye contact. Second, she was frank and straightforward—she did not readily sign on, she needed time to think. When we parted ways, we agreed to touch base in a few days, and she would let me know then whether she accepted our offer. This was a two-way street. Nancy had every right to decline the proposition, and I had every right to feel she wasn't the right fit.

The flight back to LaGuardia was a story in itself. When I arrived at the airport, the agent at the counter asked for my weight and then weighed my briefcase. Never having experienced this, I asked the agent why she did this. She replied they needed to weigh everything going on the flight.

The plane was a small eight-seater, with four seats on both sides of the aisle and one pilot (no copilot!). Everyone who boarded was asked to sit on the right side of the aisle, leaving the left-side seats open. This was a bit puzzling until a heavyset woman boarded and was directed to sit on the left side. Then it all made sense—with a small plane, the center of gravity was essential and this woman must have weighed about the same as the rest of us combined on the right-hand side.

I got home safe and sound, thinking of the old movie I saw as a little boy, *God Is My Co-Pilot*. When I got home, my wife asked how the trip was. She did not like the idea that I was on a plane without a copilot.

Nancy got in touch with me a few days after I returned from Nantucket and agreed to accept the assignment to enhance the pool. We left the question open about helping us with the rest of the search. Within a few days, I received a letter outlining the following terms of our agreement:

SCOPE OF SERVICE

Phase I

We mutually agreed to provide Gallaudet University recruiting assistance, the results of which must take place between Monday, November 16 and Thursday, November 26, 1987.

During this timeframe, we will endeavor to locate qualified candidates for the presidency. We agree to give you and Gallaudet University our best efforts to augment the existing pool of applications and nominations by plus or minus five individuals.

We will concentrate our efforts on locating qualified candidates from the hearing academic administrative and government sectors. If we happen to locate qualified hearing-impaired candidates, we will be pleased to provide these nominations as well.

We will request that candidates forward materials directly to you and will forward all nominations and materials to you as they become available. Please be aware some individuals may forward materials to us in the interest of confidentiality. All information we have will certainly be available by the time the search committee meets on December 1, 1987. You have agreed that I may attend that December 1 meeting.

Phase II [Plan A]

We agreed that should we locate candidates who are seriously considered by the committee, we will be able to assist you and the committee with further background information/checking and will assist in the communication between candidates and you as chair of the committee. (If none of our candidates are considered further, then this plan is not applicable.)

Phase II [Plan B]

If you and the search committee elect to do so, we will assist you with background checking on the serious pool of serious candidates (six, but no more than ten). (This plan is possible regardless of the outcome of Plan A, i.e., if we are considered as the appropriate organization to do so.) Whatever options you select, we are prepared to assist you with any issues/questions with which you wish advice or discussion.

This was a big relief for me. Looking back, the other two firms that I interviewed prior to Nancy's were not concerned about damage control. They wanted the opportunity, while Nancy came in from a different plane, and that was more genuine for me. Jane agreed with my choice and then had to go to the board's executive committee for final approval, which was granted.

Nancy's plan after the meeting was to move as fast as she could, considering the fact that the November 26 deadline would not be extended. Her firm would focus on getting as many nominations as possible, which, in turn, would generate applications. Sure enough, there was a rush of nominations and subsequent applications of both deaf and hearing candidates as the deadline drew near.

On November 25, I received a letter, which was copied to the board of trustees, from a large group composed of faculty and staff on campus. The letter emphasized the need for a deaf president for Gallaudet. It read as follows:

Dear Mr. Bravin:

We write as concerned faculty and staff members regarding the task now confronting your committee and the Board of Trustees: selecting, from a pool of highly qualified candidates, the individual best suited for the position of president of Gallaudet University. We are of one mind on this issue: we feel strongly that every effort should be made to appoint a highly qualified deaf person to this position.

We are sure that there will be deaf candidates as well qualified as the hearing applicants.

Accordingly, we believe that deafness should be among the
paramount considerations in deciding who will become our
next president.

Gallaudet's mission as an institution for the deaf would be
best served by having a deaf president. A deaf president would
best be able to understand and deal with the special needs and
conditions of deafness. He or she would be an inspirational role
model for deaf people everywhere, and an eloquent spokesperson on the concerns and strengths of the deaf community.
With the effective use of interpreters, a deaf president would be
able to maintain good relations with Congress and handle the
complex communications required for directing and leading a
federally supported university. Having a deaf president would
be a real "selling point" for Gallaudet, and would erase whatever
latent doubts members of Congress might have about the abilities of a deaf person.

A deaf president, now, of Gallaudet University would bring
to fruition efforts begun by Thomas Hopkins Gallaudet almost
two centuries ago.

I had received letters like this from individuals and groups,
and if they were addressed to the search committee, they were
shared with the committee. I made it a point to read every
letter in case people asked me whether I got their letter. My
stock response was, "I am almost sure I did and thank you." I
had to put the "almost" in because of the volume of letters, but
Lil Holt made sure all of them were delivered to me. If they
were addressed to the board of trustees, Lil kept them together
and put them in a book (which was over two inches thick) that
would be reviewed by the board later on when they were in
town for the final selection.

One of the letters came from Max Friedman, a member of
the class of 1932. Max was one of my earlier mentors in life.
In years past, we drove together to attend the board meetings

of the Empire State Association of the Deaf in New York. He was in his seventies then, but he always insisted on driving the four to six hours without stopping, and we chatted all the way. In his letter, he told me that "for all it is worth, my two cents' worth—if it is worth two cents . . . you and the deaf members of the committee are going to get a lot of flack if you do not pick a deaf man. But, as far as I am concerned, the very best man should be chosen."

While letters such as these reflected the collective wishes of the various constituents and individuals, the task of the committee at that time was to find the best person, deaf or hearing. The letters might have had the desired effect if a deaf candidate was borderline in terms of qualifications, placing the doubt in his or her favor and putting him or her into the interview pool. But being chair, I had absolutely no influence, and I refused to exert any influence on this except to reemphasize that our task was to narrow down the pool and submit the best candidates to the board.

The deaf press published a lot of articles and stories about Gallaudet and the presidential search process. I was interviewed by some of these publications, and I always gave my stock answers. If I strayed from these at all, my responses would be overanalyzed. If I ran into people on the street, I would get questions and again, stock answers would be the key because people would say, "I just met Phil Bravin, and he said this and that." And they would then compare notes.

7

Narrowing Down the Pool

Every search is a logistical nightmare. Measures have to be in place to ensure that all documents are protected and full confidentiality is maintained. This is necessary out of respect for those who apply. Many of the applicants for the Gallaudet presidency were executives of organizations and universities. Some were sitting college presidents who were not ready to inform their campuses back home that they were seeking a new opportunity. If the information leaked out, they theoretically would be lame ducks back home. Lil Holt was the guardian of all this and, in addition, she took care of the logistics for the search committee meetings, including arranging the candidates' travel and scheduling the interviews.

After the Thanksgiving weekend, Lil worked overtime to get everything ready for the search committee meetings from November 30 to December 2. At that time, we would whittle down the applicant pool to those who would be interviewed. Due to the upcoming holidays, we decided to conduct all the interviews in January. The exact days and times would depend on the number of candidates we would be interviewing.

By the time the search committee met on November 30, we were all glad to see each other. We had gotten to know each other, and we had begun to develop trusting relationships. There was a great level of camaraderie among the members. The requirement for confidentiality added to this because outside the committee, there was no one we could talk to regarding the search. Being together in the committee meetings was like going into a confessional—people opened up and talked about the process. We tried to keep talking about specific candidates to a minimum to reduce bias, unless there was something that needed to be brought up. Hugs upon greeting and departure were the order of the day. Reminders of the confidentiality of the process were issued every now and then.

Lil and I developed a plan to maintain the confidentiality of the committee meetings. Lil made sure that every document was numbered sequentially, which gave us the assurance that no document left the room. Even notepaper was not taken out of the room, and Lil shredded it afterward. As far as I know, this process worked well for us and, in a way, cleared my conscience and diminished the worry that leaks could happen. We were in a veritable fishbowl, with the world watching every move we made and hoping for any information that might leak out of the committee. While these procedures may seem like something out of the Central Intelligence Agency (CIA), we enforced them throughout the duration of the search. If there were notebooks at the meetings, they were also numbered and accounted for before anyone could leave the room.

When the search committee met on December 1, Nancy Archer-Martin, our search consultant, gave a status report. She told us that she had recruited sixteen candidates, all of whom had expressed initial interest and submitted their applications. She emphasized that her work was to support the committee, not to intrude or take over its role and responsibilities. She then outlined the ways that her firm could assist in the search process.[13]

Keep communication lines going between candidates you select and the committee in between meetings. Candidates are always concerned about the nature of the process and need to be kept informed about timing. That's hard for committee members to do when you all have other lives to lead besides this one. Moreover, candidates tend to tell a third party about their concerns and questions. If you know about these issues ahead of time, you can deal with them.

---

13. Nancy Archer-Martin, memorandum, December 1, 1987. Courtesy of the author's personal files.

Assist in developing an interview process which assures that you garner the same information from each candidate. Also, now that you may have some candidates in your portfolio who didn't start out looking, there are various approaches you will need to utilize to keep them from dropping out.

Participate in referencing. References do tend to be more open and honest with a third party. We believe representatives from your committee and board of trustees will want to participate in referencing, and we will work with you to coordinate that process to maintain confidentiality and yet get the information you and they will need to make an informed decision.

Assist in gathering compensation information from the final candidate(s) so that your board chair will have knowledge of any issues which may require special attention.

After Nancy's presentation, the committee got to work on screening the applications. The process worked like this: Using the three piles created by the screening subcommittee, we reviewed the rejected applications first, then the borderline applications, and, finally, the applications to be considered. Every member of the committee had the privilege of bringing up a rejected application for active consideration, so by this time, some of the applications from the rejected and borderline piles had made their way to the active consideration pile.

We then discussed each application in the active consideration pile. Oftentimes, the dynamics of the committee came into play—sometimes a random comment would shift the discussion one way or the other—but in the end, we were able to whittle the pool down to seventeen applicants from the eighty-seven applications that came in.

Nancy provided us with sample questions to ask the candidates, and we worked out a plan for who would ask them. The rotation included certain board members, the student representative, and others who represented various campus and alumni constituencies. We checked out the questions with Denise Sullivan, the head of human resources at Gallaudet and a member of the committee, to be sure they observed Equal Employment Opportunity guidelines.

After our subcommittee meetings, I suggested to Jane Spilman that we engage Nancy Archer-Martin for the rest of the search, and she agreed with me. In retrospect, Nancy and her associate were of great help to the process, and they enhanced the quality of the screening, interviewing, and final selection process.

8

The Interviews

Reality began to set in. The interviews would take place in the space of three weekends in January, and before that, we needed to prepare briefing booklets along with suggested questions for the interview committee to ask. The committee scheduled a planning meeting for late December, but because of the holidays, we pushed it to the weekend of January 9 and 10. At that time, we decided to hold the interviews on January 15, 16, and 17, and on January 22, 23, and 24, at the Grand Hyatt Hotel in downtown Washington, DC. The semifinalist interviews would take place in early February on campus.

The Grand Hyatt was ideal for us because it had space that allowed us to hide ourselves from the public. We chose the Latrobe Room on Level 3B, three floors below the main lobby and the farthest room from the elevator and stairway. The high visibility of the search in the community necessitated such action. Plus, the high-profile candidates were not yet ready to make their candidacy public, and we wanted to respect that.

Deaf people are completely dependent on visual communication, so when they participate in meetings, a bit of extra preparation is required to make sure there are clear lines of sight and good lighting in the room. Since the search committee was a mix of deaf and hearing folks, we set up the table in the room in the shape of a U. That way, the deaf members could easily see their deaf colleagues and the ASL interpreters. Normally, when there was a mixed group of deaf people and hearing people in a meeting, we had what is called a "deaf row," where the deaf people sat together and had a good line of sight to the interpreter, and the hearing people sat around that group. Because the deaf members of the committee needed to see the candidates and each other, we placed the candidates at the center of the long side of the U, and the interpreters stood behind the hearing candidates. In this arrangement, hearing and deaf candidates could maintain eye contact with everyone in the room.

Each interview followed the same ritual. I greeted the candidate outside the room to "warm" them up and to ask if they had any questions before they went in. I was sensitive to the fact that some of the hearing candidates would be meeting a deaf person for the first time and might be nervous about using an interpreter. I explained to them that while it might seem natural to look at the interpreter when they talked or when the interpreter was voicing, it was important not to do so, but to look at the committee members. Eye contact is extremely important for deaf and hearing people, and losing it could be fatal to their success. This explanation usually put them at ease before they went into the room.

I could imagine the tension and nervousness the candidates experienced when they entered the room. They were facing a group of people they had never met, and some of those strangers used a different form of communication. On top of that, since we had male and female interpreters, there could be situations where a female interpreter would voice for a male deaf person or a male interpreter would voice for a female deaf person.

The interviews usually started with some warm-up questions that had nothing to do with Gallaudet or the presidency. After several minutes, we began asking the prescripted questions listed below. These questions were quite all-encompassing in order to give the interviewee an idea of the broad variety of issues that a typical college president has to deal with. They also were designed to give us a sense of the person and, most importantly, to see if they were a good fit for Gallaudet.

In what ways is the presidency of Gallaudet College attractive to you?

Conversely, what concerns do you have about the position?

In your opinion, what particular issues will Gallaudet face in the future because of its mission as a college to serve the hearing impaired?

What do you see as the role of the faculty and the students in the governance of Gallaudet?

What familiarity do you have with sign language? Would you anticipate any difficulty in becoming proficient in sign language in a relatively short time?

What do you see as the role of the board of trustees in relationship to that of the president?

What have been your most significant achievements in your present position?

Where have you been less successful?

As you know, the college is unique in that it includes precollegiate programs. From your perspective, what are the potential benefits of this arrangement—and what are its implications for presidential leadership?

Gallaudet will be vying increasingly with other priority needs for federal support. In what ways can the president increase the understanding and support of the public about the value of Gallaudet's mission?

Would you be comfortable in working with the business community, the Congress, our alumni, etc., in seeking support for the college?

Within the context of the very special mission of Gallaudet, what would be your definition of educational quality?

How would you balance Gallaudet's internal needs for leadership against our needs to maintain a good relationship with the federal government and further cultivate individuals and organizations in the private sector?

A major function for the president of Gallaudet is to serve as an advocate for the deaf community. How would you *see* yourself in this role and do you have any tentative thoughts about how you would address this dimension of the presidency?

Assuming that the president of Gallaudet must be able to demonstrate a strong commitment to the handicapped—and most specifically the hearing impaired—what can you share with us about your experiences and relationships that would help us to understand your ability to be actively supportive of the hearing impaired?

We ended up with the linchpin question, which was drafted by Alexander Patterson. We called it the "elephant in the room" question, after the "Parable of the Elephant and the Blind Men." In that well-known story, six blind men feel different parts of an elephant, and each comes up with a different idea of what the elephant is. In our version, we asked the deaf and hearing candidates a different version of the question. First, we summarized the parable; then we asked the hearing candidates, "The deaf community fully expects the next president of Gallaudet will be deaf. If you were selected president of Gallaudet, how would you handle this situation of not fulfilling the community's expectations?" The deaf candidates got a different question: "If you were selected as the first deaf president of Gallaudet, how would you fulfill the community's expectations?"

The results were interesting and unexpected, but they made winnowing down the pool somewhat easier. Although it was not the only criterion, it was a key component of the interview. If the hearing candidates did not mention the possibility of treading into uncharted territory and not meeting the expectation of the community or how they would manage that expectation, it was a strike against them. Some completely missed the point of the enormity of this situation. If the deaf candidates indicated that being the first deaf president would be like walking into a fishbowl and that dealing with a board that never had to deal with a deaf president would be a challenge, this made a strong impression. Also, the concept of "proving" themselves as a deaf person was another key consideration. Few of the candidates, whether deaf or hearing, were able to quickly answer their respective question—most took time to ponder before giving their response.

Most of the interviews took an hour and a half to two hours. After each interview concluded, I walked out with the candidates and thanked them for their time and interest in Gallaudet. I also indicated that we would get back to them in a couple of weeks as to their status. When I went back into the room, I reminded the committee members to be consistent in their remarks should anyone in the community ask them questions about the interviews.

In yet another effort at managing confidentiality, no papers were taken out of the interview room. Lil Holt prepared a booklet on each candidate that contained their cover letter and resume/CV. The booklets were distributed to each member of the committee before the candidate entered the room, and the committee members were expected to take notes in each booklet. We allowed time prior to the interview for the committee to review the candidate's booklet, and at the end of the interview, Lil collected all the booklets. We might have gone too far in doing so, but looking back, virtually no information leaked out of the committee, and that made things easier for everyone. To this day, the identities of the seventeen candidates (except for the semifinalists) have never been revealed.

Conducting all the interviews required an enormous time commitment, but the committee members fulfilled their responsibilities faithfully. To this day, I cannot thank them enough for their dedication to the task at hand.

The search committee met again the following week to discuss the results of the seventeen interviews and to narrow down the pool to six semifinalists. For the most part, the search consultant, Nancy Archer-Martin, and I informed those who didn't make it. I have to admit that I found this task difficult. I knew some of the candidates very well; others I didn't. We used a standard script to be sure everyone was treated the same way. Sometimes a personal tone was thrown in if I knew the person well enough, and some feedback was offered if one asked for such. A typical call went like this: "Hi, this is Phil Bravin calling to discuss the results of the interview. I regret to inform you that you will not be moving to the next round of interviews. We want to thank you for your interest in Gallaudet. If you have any questions or thoughts, please feel free to share them with me." Some people would be quiet for a while before commenting. Others responded with a simple statement, like "Thanks for the opportunity to be considered." Some asked for more specific information on why they wouldn't be considered further. We then followed the calls with a letter informing them of their status.

For those who moved on to the next round, I told them, "I am pleased to inform you that you will be part of the next round of interviews, which will take place on campus. I want to thank you for your time and effort being part of a very important process for Gallaudet. Lil Holt and Nancy Archer-Martin will be in touch with you to facilitate plans for your visit to the campus." The response was usually one of elation and a "thank you."

The six semifinalists were as follows (in alphabetical order):

Dr. Harvey J. Corson, superintendent of the Louisiana School for the Deaf in Baton Rouge, Louisiana. He had an earned doctorate from the University of Cincinnati and was a former classroom teacher at Kendall School on the Gallaudet campus. He was also a Gallaudet alumnus and was a current member of the Gallaudet University Board of Trustees. (He stepped down temporarily from the board when he decided to be a candidate for the presidency of Gallaudet.)

Dr. Robert R. Davila, vice president of precollege programs at Gallaudet. He had earned a doctorate from Syracuse University. Like Dr. Corson, he started his career as a classroom teacher at the New York School for the Deaf and was a Gallaudet alumnus.

Dr. William R. Dill, president of Babson College in Wellesley, Massachusetts. He had received a doctorate from Carnegie Mellon University. He had been a Fulbright Scholar and dean of the Graduate School of Business at New York University.

Dr. I. King Jordan, dean of the College of Arts and Sciences at Gallaudet. He graduated from Gallaudet and then obtained a doctorate from the University of Tennessee. He returned to the Gallaudet campus as a professor in the Department of Psychology until he became dean in 1986.

Dr. Humphrey R. Tonkin, president of the State University of New York at Potsdam. British born, he graduated from Cambridge University and received a doctorate from Harvard University. He was a linguist and a recognized expert on Esperanto.

Dr. Elisabeth A. Zinser, vice chancellor for Academic Affairs at the University of North Carolina, Greensboro. She was a graduate of Stanford University and had a doctorate from the University of California, Berkeley. She also received an MBA from the MIT Sloan School of Management.

All told, there were three deaf candidates—Corson, Davila, and Jordan. Each of the hearing candidates had, in my opinion, a thread that led them to Gallaudet. Dill had worked at IBM and knew Gustave Rathe, who was on the search committee. Tonkin, an expert on languages, had a good understanding of ASL from a linguistic point of view but wasn't a fluent signer. He was an expert on Esperanto, which is considered the most widely spoken constructed international auxiliary language. This gave him insight into ASL and deaf culture. Zinser spent most of her early years in the medical and educational professions.

Of the deaf candidates, I knew Corson very well. In addition to being a colleague of mine on the Gallaudet board, he had been two years ahead of me in college. I was the secretary of the SBG at Gallaudet while he was the president. I met Davila for the first time when I enrolled at the New York School for the Deaf. I was eight years old, and he was a first-year teacher. While he never taught me, he was an advisor to some of the student organizations I joined. In addition, our paths had crossed several times in the deaf community. I knew Jordan very casually. I had met him for the first time in the boardroom when he was introduced as the dean of the College of Arts and Sciences at Gallaudet. The degrees of separation in the deaf community are much smaller than in the hearing community.

The search committee started planning for the on-campus interviews for the six semifinalists. To give everyone a fair shake in preparation for the interviews, I asked Nancy to offer all the candidates the opportunity to ask me any questions they might have about Gallaudet or deafness. Only Elisabeth Zinser took me up on this offer. Lil Holt made arrangements for me and an interpreter to fly to Greensboro. I decided to bring one of the interpreters we used during the first round of interviews because she was familiar with Zinser and could interpret the subtleties of her speech.

I met Dr. Zinser on her campus, and we walked over to the library for a chat. She was well prepared for our session and asked very thought-provoking questions. I wanted to be fair to all the remaining candidates, so I was careful not to give her any information that she could use to her advantage in upcoming interviews. However, since the other two hearing semifinalists did not ask to meet with me, I sometimes wonder if I inadvertently gave her some extra help. I could understand why the deaf semifinalists did not need to ask any questions, but I've always been puzzled about why Dr. Dill and Dr. Tonkin did not take the opportunity when it was offered.

Various constituencies in the deaf world learned of my trip to North Carolina, and they screamed bloody murder, claiming that I gave Zinser an advantage. A rumor also circulated that Jerry Lee and Jane Spilman had driven down to Greensboro to meet with Zinser, and this was true. Sean Piccoli, a reporter for the *Washington Times*, requested an interview with me for an article about the search process, which I granted. The article appeared in the *Washington Times* on March 2. He asked me about my meeting with Zinser, as well as Lee and Spilman's trip to North Carolina. I told him that we had informed all six semifinalists that they would be invited to the campus for more interviews in February and that all of them could contact me if they had further questions or if they desired information.

I also told Piccoli that Elisabeth Zinser had a great many questions that "could not be practically handled over the phone. And this was why I made the trip to North Carolina, to answer all the questions and the other things she needed to know. She asked to meet with Dr. Lee and Mrs. Jane Bassett Spilman (chair of the trustees). There were questions that were obviously not in the realm of my knowledge." Lee and Spilman met with Zinser the following day, and "if other candidates had requested the same, to meet with myself, Dr. Lee, and Mrs. Spilman, they would have been extended the same courtesy. One of the ground rules of the search committee was that each of the candidates is to be treated equally."[14] Since I could not share every action I took with the public, the role of the press here was helpful. (This visit by Lee and Spilman was also verified by Elisabeth Zinser in a separate interview in November 1991 after the movement.)[15]

After my visit to North Carolina, Nancy Archer-Martin started the process of doing final background checks on the semifinalists. This was a process best left to the professionals in the field, like her. She obtained as much information as possible to create a profile of each candidate for the committee

---

14. Sean Piccoli, "Gallaudet Rally Calls for Deaf President," *Washington Times*, March 2, 1988.

15. Elizabeth Zinser, "Dr. Elisabeth Zinser: Breaking the Silence," *Deaf Life*, November 1991.

and board to review down the road. She even included a list of comments, both pros and cons, on each candidate, so we could get a complete picture.

Spilman sent a letter to the board of trustees, updating them on the search process and informing them that the finalist interviews would occur on March 5 and 6. The regular meeting of the board was to take place on March 7. She then said, "[I]t is a demanding schedule but eminently vital to our University. I urge each of you to make every effort to attend and participate in the entire program. The search committee has labored long and arduously and given unselfishly of their time. Now is the time for the board to respond in kind."

Up until then, the search process had been as airtight as possible. None of the candidates' names had been made public, but now it was time to release that information. After the names were made public, Lil told me that the campus started to buzz with activity, and the watercoolers were more crowded than usual.

Lil, Nancy, and I started to plan for the on-campus interviews. The candidates would be meeting with eight different campus groups, and we had to figure out a way to not skew the opinions of each group. The candidates would be interviewed in close order, and we didn't want the interview of the first candidate to influence the results of the successive ones. We tried to create a wall around each candidate's interview within each group.

Each of the following groups was asked to select representatives for the on-campus interviews:

- President's Council on Deafness: An elected group of deaf faculty and staff members
- Staff Advisory Committee: Members of the staff (non-faculty) on campus
- University Faculty Senate: Elected leaders of the faculty

- Alumni: Officers and representatives of the Gallaudet University Alumni Association
- Student Body Representatives: Selected members of the SBG (undergraduate) and the Graduate Student Association (graduate students)
- Central Administration: Administrators reporting to the president
- Council of Deans: All the deans on campus (educational administrators)
- Precollege Faculty: Representatives from the Kendall Demonstration Elementary School and Model Secondary School for the Deaf

The rules were such that each group was required to submit their recommendations/feedback to the search committee no later than twenty-four hours after their interviews. If they failed to meet the deadline, their recommendations would not be used. We did this to prevent a group from modifying their recommendations for an earlier candidate after interviewing other candidates. We also made sure that if each group had questions or concerns during the interviews, Lil and I would be available to respond to them. This process worked very well and reduced the element of bias to a much lower degree. It should be noted that no group failed to meet the twenty-four-hour requirement.

The next step was to plan the candidates' time on campus. We made sure that the interviewees always had someone to keep them company, that they had some personal time for reflection, and that their personal needs were met. The bottom line was we wanted to sell Gallaudet to the candidates as much as the candidates were selling themselves to Gallaudet. Finally, we had to make sure that the candidates did not bump into each other. We assigned a person to take each candidate from one interview to the next. We also scheduled the interviews on different parts of the campus, so that the candidates could see the full extent of the university's property.

All the interviews took place over a ten-day period, and each candidate spent a full day on campus. Each candidate was offered the option to bring their spouse or partner to campus. The schedule for each candidate on the eve of the interviews was something like this:

- Tour of the Northwest campus.
- Dinner at House One with some members of the search committee. There was no formal agenda, but the dinner gave the committee members an opportunity to observe the social graces of the candidates, since entertaining is a key aspect of the president's job.
- Lil Holt and I gave each candidate and their spouse/partner a tour of House One, answering questions they might have of their potential future residence and, at the same time, relating some historical aspects of the house and Gallaudet itself. While the spouse/partner was not a determinant in the decision-making process, his or her participation was welcome.

The following day, we scheduled a tour of the main campus for the spouse, if that was requested, while the candidates were interviewed. I met with each candidate individually to go over the agenda for the day. Then, I brought the candidate to the first interview session, and a representative from each group took the candidate to the following interview session. There was also a lunch with the Central Administration and the Federal Relations Liaison. At the end of the day, the local search group, which was composed of members of the search committee who resided in the Washington, DC, area, met with the candidate to wrap things up and to answer any outstanding questions before they left campus.

Six formal dinners and campus tours in a short number of days, along with the logistics involved, created a pressure cooker atmosphere, but we sailed through that without a hitch; Lil was a great captain throughout the whole process. We finished with all the interviews on Tuesday, February 16, 1988. After that, Lil gathered the feedback from each of the campus groups and from individuals who had submitted their comments. In all, we had forty-eight portfolios to deal with (six candidates, eight campus groups). Lil prepared a set of portfolios, each averaging seven pages, for every member of the search committee, a total of 624 portfolios. Of course, all of this had to be done in full secrecy, and the information had to be very secure. We also numbered each document to ensure we could account for all the copies.

I wrote letters to the campus groups, thanking them for their participation. The flurry of letters did not distract me from focusing on the main task at hand mainly because Lil helped keep me on track while working out the details for the next stage of the process. We were getting into the final stretch. The next step would be the last meeting of the search committee to reduce the pool, if necessary, before recommending the finalists to the board.

9

Selecting the President amid Mounting Public Pressure

The search committee met again on Saturday and Sunday, February 27–28, 1988, to go over the results of the campus interviews and decide which candidates we would recommend to the board. Each of the committee members had a portfolio of each candidate in front of them, consisting of the following:

- The cover letter submitted by the candidate at the time they expressed their interest
- The resume (CV) of the candidate
- The results of the on-campus interviews from each group
- The background checks performed by Nancy Archer-Martin

On Sunday, we had our final deliberations and chose three finalists to recommend to the board: Dr. Harvey J. Corson (deaf), Dr. I. King Jordan (deaf), and Dr. Elisabeth A. Zinser (hearing). We had fulfilled our responsibility, and so the committee disbanded.

Based on informal conversations I had with members of the deaf community at large, I got the sense that the community seemed to think that as the chair, I had some influence or say in the search process and the deliberations of the search committee. This was the farthest thing from the truth. My function was to manage the search to a conclusion; the committee was the final arbiter for the semifinalists, not me. My role was to shepherd the process to find the best person to lead Gallaudet. Our discussions as a whole were not contentious, and the decisions were often made with a comfortable majority, a reflection of the quality of the work and documentation we received. It was now up to the board of trustees, of which I was a member, to interview the finalists and select the new president.

In the days leading up to the board of trustee's meeting, the campus came alive with speculation. The level of anticipation resulted in more public attention, along with a growing influx of letters to me and Jane Spilman. We received letters from public figures as well as various stakeholders in the community, including Vice President George H. W. Bush and Senators Bob Dole (R-KS), Lowell Weicker (R-CT), Tom Harkin (D-IA), and Bob Graham (D-FL). Vice President Bush wrote, in part, "Gallaudet has a responsibility to set an example and thus to appoint a president who is not only highly qualified, but who is also deaf. I hope that the trustees will keep Gallaudet's critical leadership position in mind when they make their decision."

In addition to letters, articles and editorials started to appear in the papers. On February 22, Dorothy Gilliam, a well-respected African American journalist at the *Washington Post*, wrote an editorial in which she said, "Gallaudet hiring a hearing-impaired president would make a great statement to people who are handicapped throughout the United States, that disability will in no way disable them from attaining their goals and that our democracy is rich enough to afford the diversity. My own view is that from great institutions great things are expected. Wouldn't it be great if Gallaudet rises to the challenge?"[16]

Dr. Edward C. Merrill, the fourth president of Gallaudet, wrote a letter to Jane Spilman on February 26, after he saw the announcement of the six semifinalists, three of whom were deaf. The letter was thoughtful and powerful, apart from being an impassioned plea for a deaf president. He began by saying,

> Since concluding my term of office as the fourth president of Gallaudet in October 1983, I have been gratified with the

---

16. In 1988, *hearing impaired* was the generally accepted term to describe people who did not hear. Today, however, *deaf* (or *hard of hearing*) is the preferred term, and it also describes our community and culture. Dorothy Gilliam, "A President for Gallaudet," *Washington Post*, February 22, 1988.

continued progress of the institution. Dr. Lee has been an astute leader, and the board of trustees has acted wisely in supporting his administration. I am writing to you now because I am still deeply interested in Gallaudet University and the clientele it serves.

From my perspective, having purposefully removed myself from the affairs of the university for the past few years, the university now faces a moment of truth as it always does when a new president must be named. On this occasion, however, the three deaf candidates as well as the hearing candidates are exceptionally well qualified. To what extent, then, is the element of deafness to be weighed in the selection of a president to serve a deaf student body and a deaf national constituency? Two developments may shed some light on this issue. One development is the historical evolution of social institutions, and the other development is a well established psychological principle that functions in groups and institutions in modern society.

Merrill then summarized the history of deaf education and special education in the United States, and he talked about the work of minority groups to achieve fair and equal treatment. He concluded by stating:

I am sure that the success of Gallaudet, especially its university status so aptly provided by Dr. Lee and the Congress, would surpass [Edward Miner Gallaudet's] remotest dreams. He could not imagine the positive impact of the institution he established in opening the doors of education everywhere and at all levels to deaf persons with correlative developments in employment, civic involvement, and even political action. The greatest compliment to him and to those who followed him, including Dr. Lee and me, would be to know that Gallaudet University was still a pioneer in the education of the deaf—under the leadership of a deaf person.

It was unusual for such a small university like Gallaudet to garner national attention during a search. Yes, this was an

THE VICE PRESIDENT
WASHINGTON

March 1, 1988

Mr. Philip Bravin
Presidential Search Committee
Gallaudet University
7th and Florida Avenue, NE
Washington, DC 20002

Dear Mr. Bravin:

It is my understanding that Gallaudet University is in the process of selecting a new President. I also understand that you have identified six finalists who are highly qualified for the position, three of whom are deaf.

I have a deep interest in disability civil rights. Over the past few years I have worked with many national and local organizations run by and for disabled people, including the National Council on Independent Living, the National Council on the Handicapped, Capitol People First of Sacramento and the Association on Handicapped Student Service Programs in Post-Secondary Education. I have also had many conversations with disabled leaders, including deaf persons, throughout the United States. And my office has served as the focal point for the development of the Administration's disability policy.

From this experience, I have become aware of the two basic principles that underly the disability rights movement; the right of disabled people to control their own lives and the right to integration and involvement in society.

Gallaudet University has a critical role to play in advancing these principles. It is held in the highest regard by deaf people throughout the United States and the world. It provides an excellent education and a meaningful future for thousands of deaf persons. More importantly, Gallaudet University is a symbol of leadership and opportunity, not only for deaf people, but for all of us.

In the last two decades our society has undergone a quiet revolution. The Congress, the Courts and the Administration have strongly supported the right of people with disabilities to hold positions of trust and leadership. Our government has enacted numerous laws to ensure that disabled people are ensured equality of opportunity.

Accordingly, as an entity funded by the Federal government, Gallaudet has a responsiblity to set an example and thus to appoint a President who is not only highly qualified, but who is also deaf. I hope that the Trustees will keep Gallaudet's critical leadership position in mind when they make their decision.

Sincerely,

George Bush

Letter from Vice President George H. W. Bush, who was running for the US presidency in 1988. The primary elections (Super Tuesday) took place during the week of DPN. Courtesy of the author's personal files.

United States Senate

COMMITTEE ON LABOR AND
HUMAN RESOURCES

WASHINGTON, DC 20510

Subcommittee on the Handicapped
113 Hart Senate Office Building
Washington, D.C. 20510

February 29, 1988

Mr. Philip Bravin, Chairman
Presidential Search Committee
Gallaudet University
7th and Florida Avenue, N.E.
Washington, D.C. 20002

Dear Mr. Bravin,

It has come to our attention that the Presidential Search Committee at Gallaudet University, through a comprehensive examination, has narrowed the number of candidates to six, three of whom are deaf.

We understand and support the efforts by the Search Committee to choose the candidate who will best serve the needs of Gallaudet University. Consistent with this effort, it is our hope that you will give due consideration to the principle of taking affirmative action to employ and promote qualified deaf individuals into positions of authority and responsibility. The selection of a highly qualified deaf individual to the presidency would certainly be a powerful reaffirmation of Gallaudet's commitment to the principle of affirmative action.

Thank you for your thoughtful consideration of this matter.

Sincerely,

Lowell P. Weicker, Jr.
Ranking Minority Member

Tom Harkin
Chairman

TH/LW/kb

Letter from Senators Weicker (R-CT) and Harkin (D-IA). Note that it was a bipartisan letter. Courtesy of the author's personal files.

election year in the United States, but the attention nevertheless was telling of how the rest of the world viewed the search. Even a Harvard search would not draw the same attention from politicians. Credit for this goes to the deaf community, who used their representatives in Congress and the national political parties to drive home the message of how important it was to select a deaf president. The letters kept pouring in, and I tried my best to keep up with them, but of course, I couldn't respond to them all. If I did, it might cause members of the community to read between the lines, which would likely generate more letters.

In one of my last acts as chair of the PSC, I decided not to share any of the letters with the other members of the committee. We had worked hard to focus on the qualifications of the candidates and their compatibility with Gallaudet, nothing more, nothing less. I thought it was important to avoid any outside or political bias; I still feel strongly this was the right decision to insulate the committee from any political influences. Anything political or otherwise was best left to the board. The letters, including Merrill's (which I had not seen by the final meeting of the search committee), were put in binders to be shared with the board members before they gathered for the final selection meeting. In the meantime, we went home.

A rally in support of a deaf president took place on the Gallaudet campus on March 1 while I was in Dallas on IBM business. Of course, the community had a right to express its opinion in the hopes that it would affect the board's decision. It did organize the community for what was to come. In addition, since the media covered it, the rally participants were able to get their message of "it's time for a deaf president" out to the general public.

From the outset of the search process, the deaf members of the board—myself, Robert Sanderson, and Frank Sullivan—had a gentleman's agreement never to use the hint of or an actual protest as a way of forcing the selection of a deaf person. We wanted the president, if he or she were deaf, to be selected on his or her merits, not because of a threat of a protest. However, the press did its job. News of the rally appeared on local television stations and in local papers, but most of the board members lived out of town. Remember, this was 1988. If the

3-1-88

```
------------------------------Speech----------------------------
     Greetings! My name is Terry Giansanti. I am 12 years old and

a student at Kendall School. I am happy to be here to share my

thoughts with you about having a deaf president for Gallaudet

University.

     It is very important that Gallaudet has a deaf president. A

deaf president makes an excellent role model for children at

Kendall and all other schools for the deaf. Deaf children can

develop a more positive attitude about reaching high career goals

like being President of Gallaudet or any other corporation or

even becoming a politician.

     Having a deaf President can break barriers. For example,

communications will be easier. Another example, a deaf president

already understands the culture and life of the deaf people of

Gallaudet and also in the deaf community all over the USA and the

world. A deaf president will understand and feel our wants and

needs, and nurse them.

     All the students at KDES including myself are hoping for a

deaf president for Gallaudet University. We think it is time for

a deaf president.

     If a deaf person is chosen, finally in 124 years of the

history of Gallaudet, we can boast a deaf president.

     Thank you.

3/1/88
```

A letter written at the time of the March 1 rally by a twelve-year-old Kendall student, Terry Giansanti. He is currently the owner of a travel agency catering to deaf clients, Hands On Travel. Courtesy of the author's personal files.

rally had taken place today, the situation would have been very different; the news would have spread through social media and probably would have gone viral.

In any event, during my stay in Dallas, Molly Sinclair, a reporter from the *Washington Post* whom I got to know more down the road, left a note for me to call her back. I had trained myself to think that if I took care of the media, it would take good care of me. I called her back on the TTY through a relay service, and she asked me if I was aware of the rally. I responded yes, and then she asked me if I knew that my son participated in the rally. My oldest son, Jeff, was a freshman at Gallaudet at that time. My response was simply, "My son is now a college student, and my wife and I have decided to respect his independence as an evolving adult. He will need to learn about the results of his actions as he evolves." We have applied the same dictum to our other children, Deb and Seth, who subsequently attended Gallaudet. In my frequent trips to campus, I always made it a point to let my kids know in advance when I would be on campus, never surprising them. I then asked Molly, "If you had a child in college under similar circumstances, what would you do?" Silence then prevailed, and we went on to other subjects.

Molly wanted to know the results of the search and the process going forward. I told her that "the search had concluded and that the committee had disbanded. The committee had recommended three finalists to the board as part of fulfilling its original charge from the board. As for the rally on campus, it was the right of those to express their thoughts. The board will be interviewing the finalists next week, and we will then make the announcement at that time." This call essentially brought the facts of the process up to date. Molly became the main reporter of the developments going forward, and she did a commendable job in her reporting.

I thought to myself after the call, *The heat is starting to build, and the media has its ears pointed on this. The next few days or weeks are bound to be interesting.* I was also awed by the fact that Molly was able to track me down at a hotel in Dallas.

Maintaining a neutral stance was very important to me—people inside and outside the university were watching every move I made, trying to read between the lines of what I said in letters, interviews, and informal chats, and trying to extrapolate and speculate from all my activities. As a deaf person, I was also mindful that sign language could be picked up from one corner of a room to another. One can hear a spoken conversation from six to ten feet away, while one can see a signed conversation 50 feet away with good eyesight. So, I stopped having private conversations in a public space. I also learned to be as unobtrusive as possible when I used an ASL interpreter to talk to a hearing person.

The critical phase was nearing, and the planning had to be done in such a way that the board's selection could be made public as soon as possible. In addition, we needed to go over some campus security issues. Jane Spilman and I met with the Gallaudet public relations (PR) staff to go over the press releases that would be distributed on the day of the announcement. It was an interesting exercise. We had to draft press releases for each of the three finalists, so that we would be ready for whoever was selected. The press releases included quotes from me and Jane along with a biography of the respective candidates. Contrary to many releases, we did not ask the finalists to give us some quotes. We agreed to print 5000 copies each of the three releases. We also instructed the PR staff to destroy the other copies when we announced the new president.

One would think we would need to do all this at the time of the announcement, but because of the high level of interest and anticipation on campus and in the deaf community, we wanted to release the news immediately after the selection. We also had to make arrangements for the announcements to be secured in a safe location, one the PR staff could get to quickly and easily.

After we worked out all the details of the announcement, we met with Herb Emerson, director of security, along with his boss, Jim Barnes, the vice president of business and administration at Gallaudet. We discussed what might happen on campus when the press releases were distributed. They thought there might be some commotion, but they believed it would be manageable. I even brought up the possibility of a small protest if we chose the hearing candidate and asked how we would handle that. I told them, "We might have a protest, but I wouldn't think it would be so big as to be unmanageable; but should we have the DC police on standby and have some training for them?" My request for informing and training DC police was shot down. Herb felt the campus security folks could handle things, and Jane and Jim sided with Herb, so I backed down.

The next order of business was to meet with each candidate to go over the terms and conditions of the position before the selection. We needed to discuss the starting date of the job, the salary range, the benefits (such as living in House One, health insurance, and retirement planning, vacation time, etc.). Honestly, I would have never thought of doing this, but Nancy Archer-Martin was very strong on this. She pointed out that if we made an offer before setting the terms and conditions, the candidate could theoretically delay the announcement while we negotiated.

Jane Spilman, Jim Barnes, and I met with each of the three finalists to discuss the terms of their potential employment. Jim took notes and then drafted a memorandum of understanding to be used as a basis for negotiation by the executive committee of the board after the announcement. This was really Jane's area of responsibility as chair. I was there in a supporting role since I was not a member of the executive committee. I also had a level of understanding with the candidates since I was their main point of contact all along. Our discussions went very well, and each of the candidates was reasonable in their expectations.

The next step was to prepare for the board of trustees meeting. Each of the candidates would be interviewed in short order, and we had to make sure they did not see each other.

Harvey Corson and Elisabeth Zinser were coming in from out of town, so we put them up in separate hotels. Lil Holt made the reservations and arranged for the hotel rooms where the interviews would take place. On top of that, she scheduled the interpreters and planned meals for the board. Finally, we made profile books on each candidate for each member of the board for the interviews, like we did for the search committee. We also put all the letters we had received into two very thick binders for the board members to read.

The trustees started coming into town on Friday, March 3, and we all stayed at the Kendall apartments. That evening, there was a candlelight vigil outside the apartments in support of a deaf president. It was a beautiful sight—hundreds of candles flickering on the parking lot and the hill beyond. I felt for those out there; one part of me wanted to join them. They were my community after all; but I had to do my duty. It was definitely a struggle for me to reconcile my feelings as a deaf person with my role as a board member, and to not let my feelings sway me from doing what was best for Gallaudet.

By that time, by being very involved with the search, going through eighty-seven applicants, conducting seventeen interviews, and working with the semifinalists, I had a pretty good grasp of what Gallaudet needed and deserved. The caliber of people that we interviewed, deaf and hearing, was impressive. However, I had a strong feeling, coupled with the collective knowledge and feedback of the past several months, that it was time for a deaf president. Still, I wanted to keep my mind open in case the deaf finalists did not meet my expectations during their respective interviews.

PART TWO

THE WEEK THE WORLD
HEARD GALLAUDET

1

The Finale that Never Was a Finale: March 5–6

We were getting to the finish line—seven months had elapsed since the Vermont phone call from Jane Spilman. The interviews were set to begin at 9:00 a.m. on March 5, at the Willard Intercontinental Hotel in the Douglas Room on the second floor. Prior to the first interview, Jane Spilman came up to me and said, "Phil, since you did very well managing the interview process during the search, would you like to conduct the final interviews?" This took me a bit aback—one part of me was wondering whether it was a ploy to neutralize me, so I would not be able to ask questions; the other part of me was thinking that Jane didn't feel comfortable managing the process. I thought a while and responded by saying, "Jane, for the past seven months, I have done my best to be neutral as the chair of the search, and my mission then was to find the best candidates for Gallaudet. I want the opportunity to remove my neutral hat and put on my board hat and ask questions that will ultimately help me decide who would be the best candidate for Gallaudet." Jane replied, "Fair enough, I'll do my best."

I shared this exchange with the other deaf trustees, Robert Sanderson and Frank Sullivan, who also felt it was an attempt to neutralize the deaf wing, but we were cohesive in ensuring that the process was as fair as it could be. We kept our minds open as to whether the chosen candidate needed to be deaf or not, but there was no question that our tendencies (and hope) leaned toward a deaf candidate, subject to the interviews that were to follow.

The Douglas Room was narrow and long, with a dark wooden table in the middle and chairs ringed around it.

This was not an ideal setting for the interviews, especially if the interviewees and interpreters were at the head of the table. Robert, Frank, and I usually sat together to easily see the ASL interpreters and the interviewee, so we decided to seat the interviewee in the middle of the table, at the widest point. One of the interpreters would stand behind the hearing candidate so that the three of us had a direct line of sight to both of them. When we interviewed the deaf candidates, another interpreter stood behind us, so that the deaf candidate would be able to see the interpreter interpreting the questions/comments from the hearing board members.

Once we were seated, we discussed the protocol for the interviews. Jane suggested that we should be consistent in our questions for the three finalists, with minor deviations based on the responses. We also decided not to discuss our reactions or opinions until we had interviewed all the candidates. Lastly, each board member received the profile books that Lil Holt had prepared.

At 9:00 a.m., I. King Jordan came into the room and was introduced to the board. After we exchanged pleasantries, we began to ask our questions in no particular order, except that we started with general warm-up questions, like "What drew you to apply for this position?" and "What do you see as the unique characteristics of Gallaudet?" We then moved on to questions of a more substantive nature, such as "What is your vision for Gallaudet?" "Where do you see Gallaudet ten years from now?" "What would be your immediate challenges?" "What would your first 100 days be like?" Sometimes, we asked follow-up questions as a result of King's answers. The whole session lasted close to two hours, at the end of which we thanked Jordan for his time.

We went to lunch after Jordan's interview and came back at 1:00 p.m. to interview Elisabeth Zinser. The interview went fine, but afterward, Frank approached Jane to tell her he thought she had been overly gracious to Zinser, more so than she was with Jordan. Jane was quite surprised and denied doing that. But, basically, she was put on notice that the interview process needed to be as neutral as possible. I sensed some discomfort on her part the rest of the day as well as when we met for dinner at House One.

We regrouped the next day in the Massachusetts Room of the Mayflower Hotel for the final interview and to choose the seventh president of Gallaudet. The first order of business was interviewing Harvey Corson. We all knew him because he had been a board member until he applied for the presidency, but we did not treat him any differently from the other two finalists.

After the interview with Corson, the board took a break. Robert, Frank, and I met in private to reaffirm among ourselves that we, as the only deaf members of the board, would not even mention the threat of a protest if the deliberations resulted in a consensus that a hearing person was indeed the proper and best choice. When the board regrouped to begin discussing the finalists, Charles Haskell, a known protégé of Jane, made an unexpected motion to "allow the chair to participate in the selection process of the seventh president." I was quite surprised at this because the chair usually does not participate in discussions that result in a vote. Robert, who was a parliamentarian at heart, told Frank and myself to let this go and not make a big deal of this. Only one board member abstained from voting on this, while everyone else was for it. I decided that if any impropriety or diversion from neutrality occurred, I would not hesitate to bring it up. However, this never happened.

Haskell then introduced a second motion "to allow the chair to vote for the seventh president only in the case of a tie." I suspected this was an attempt to neutralize his previous motion. In normal parliamentary procedure, the chair does not vote unless there is a tie, so the motion was unnecessary. But we were choosing a new president, and perhaps Haskell wanted to be sure this was a ground rule. Again, the vote was 13–1, with one abstention.

The discussion then turned to the three finalists. After some review and discussion, the board decided to focus on the remaining two candidates, Zinser and Jordan.

After breaking for lunch, we reconvened, and our discussion went on at great length. We reviewed the feedback from the campus community and the search committee, Zinser's and Jordan's resumes, and the results of their respective interviews. The discussion at this point focused on what Gallaudet really needed and on the strengths and the challenges of both finalists. The subject of being deaf or not was not a centerpiece of this discussion at all—it was on the merits of Zinser and Jordan and what they could contribute to Gallaudet.

Near the end of the day, after we had been meeting for three or four hours, Thomas Penfield Jackson raised his hand and asked to address the group. This was our normal procedure; it allowed everyone, deaf and hearing, to have an opportunity to speak/sign. Without this protocol, the deaf board members would have had a difficult time jumping into a discussion. Spilman recognized Jackson, and he went into a lengthy discourse. Jackson was a federal judge, and he had a way of distilling information in a well-reasoned manner, one that made it easier for the board to make decisions. His speech on March 6 was no exception.

Jackson stood up (instead of sitting down as board members normally did) and started his discourse. While there aren't any notes from this meeting, the gist of his speech went as follows:

> Here we have an interesting situation. We have one candidate who is hearing, and another candidate who is deaf, and we have to make a choice between the two of them.
>
> Looking at the hearing candidate, we have a person who has proven herself as a college administrator and has moved up through the ranks. Her references and interview feedback have been very commendable, but she has a drawback—she has almost no background in the deaf community, nor does she have a strong understanding of deaf culture and its related aspects.

We have a deaf finalist who has been a popular professor and also a popular figure on campus but has only recently become an administrator, and he has little, if any proven management experience. But, he is deaf and has all the necessary exposure and understanding of deafness and the cultural aspects related to deafness. The question then before us is: Which candidate would require less time (or be a "quicker study" in his words, which I recall vividly) learning and understanding the issues related to deafness and making decisions on behalf of the university related to deafness, or developing the necessary management skills and techniques that are necessary in running the university. These questions relate to both candidates, and I offer the opinion that we should vote based on those premises.

This was the first time in the deliberations that the subject of being deaf was raised as a point of discussion. I was aghast and knew at that moment what Jackson really meant. It takes years for a hearing person to understand and appreciate all the issues related to deafness. Being a board member and coming to campus three to five times a year does not necessarily make a hearing person able to appreciate deafness in its myriad forms. By the same token, no one can become a manager overnight. It takes years to develop into an effective administrator. I knew, as did Robert and Frank, that an encyclopedic explanation would not do justice to "deafness" as a culture. One would have to live and breathe in the community to understand and appreciate deafness. As Willard Madsen, the deaf poet, wrote, in part,

> What is it like to be deaf and alone
> In the company of those who can hear—
> And you only guess as you go along,
> For no one's there with a helping hand,
> As you try to keep up with words and song?
> You have to be deaf to understand.[1]

---

1. Jack R. Gannon, *Deaf Heritage: A Narrative History of Deaf America* (Washington, DC: Gallaudet University Press, 2012), 380.

This is what Zinser didn't have, but Jordan did. I knew immediately then that the hearing members of the board would feel they were well grounded in deafness; they had been on the board for a number of years, but none of them, with the exception of Laurel Glass, associated with deaf people away from Gallaudet, nor could they sign. As Robert, Frank, and I had agreed earlier, we did not raise the possibility of a protest if Jordan were selected; we wanted a fair shake for Jordan and did not want the threat of a protest to be a reason for selecting the first deaf president.

Privately, I didn't know Jordan that well, but I saw potential in him and felt that he was the best person for Gallaudet. While Zinser was a commendable candidate, I thought the time was right for a deaf person, and Jordan, despite his limited management experience, had enormous potential because he was an intelligent, well-rounded person, eager and passionate, ready, willing, and able to rise to the occasion.

All the years of oppression (intentional and unintentional) by hearing people over deaf people needed to end, and we needed to prove to the world that a deaf person could lead our university. From my point of view, considering everything, I. King Jordan was what Gallaudet needed and deserved at that point in time. With the benefit of 20/20 hindsight, I don't think Robert, Frank, and I would have done anything differently. We said that the time was right for a deaf president and that Jordan was fit for the position. But, Jackson's reasoning was easy for the hearing members to comprehend and use as justification for their vote.

When Jackson finished his statement, we continued discussing the merits of each finalist. After a short while, one of the board members made a motion to conduct the vote by secret ballot and have the executive committee count the votes. The motion passed, and we began to vote.

It was 5:15 p.m. when the results were announced. Zinser received ten votes and Jordan received four. I was disappointed and, in a "whispered" conversation (signing unobtrusively, so the interpreter did not voice for us), I asked Robert and Frank

I. King Jordan's View

New to me and very important to my understanding of how the board reached the point where they voted 10–4 was the speech that trustee Thomas Penfield Jackson made during the meeting. In brief, he made the point that the decision the board was about to make was about whether it would be easier for someone with extensive administrative experience but virtually no knowledge of deafness or sign language to effectively assume the presidency over someone with extensive knowledge of deafness and sign language but limited administrative experience. What he did was wrong. What the board did was wrong. I have been a deaf man for more than fifty years, and I am still learning about deafness, deaf culture, and sign language. It sure didn't take me that long to learn to become president.

who they voted for. They both said King, and we suspected that Laurel Glass was the fourth vote. We asked her across the table in ASL without the interpreter voicing for us, "Did you vote for King?" and she signed "yes." Jane Spilman asked the board to make the vote unanimous, but the four of us said no. My heart sank to my foot, but I maintained my composure, not knowing what the rest of the day and the time to come would look like. A motion then was made to express the board's thanks and gratitude to the PSC and Lil Holt for producing a wealth of finalists for the board to consider.

It was late in the afternoon when the board adjourned. Reporters were milling around the hall outside the meeting room, but we had several things to do before dealing with the public. Of course, notifying the candidates and then issuing the press release regarding the selection was the first order of business. Jane and I discussed who should make the call to Elisabeth Zinser to break the news. Jane felt I should be the one, and we agreed that she would take over after I gave Zinser the news. I got an interpreter to facilitate the call, which went something like this:

> "Hi Elisabeth, this is Phil Bravin speaking through an interpreter. I am delighted to inform you that you have been selected as the seventh president of Gallaudet."
>
> Elisabeth responded by saying, "I am so delighted, and I look forward to the opportunity."

I then told her I would be turning the phone over to Jane. Since I was by Jane's side with an ASL interpreter throughout the call, I knew she offered her congratulations and explained some of the formalities and logistics, like mentioning the distribution of the press release and arranging for Elisabeth to be interviewed by the press after we notified the other finalists. What did not come out during the whole phone call was the fact that the vote was not unanimous. Jane did not bring it up, nor did Elisabeth broach the subject, even though she had said in a previous meeting that she would appreciate knowing this. Whether this was a strong condition of her accepting the position was never tested.

After Jane talked to Zinser, I called Harvey Corson and I. King Jordan on the TTY to inform them that they didn't make it. The conversation went something like this:

Jordan: HI THIS IS KING. GA

Bravin: GOOD AFTERNOON. THIS IS PHIL. I REGRET TO INFORM YOU THAT YOU HAVE NOT BEEN SELECTED AS THE PRESIDENT OF GALLAUDET. THE BOARD HAS APPOINTED ELISABETH ZINSER AS THE SEVENTH PRES-IDENT OF GALLAUDET. GA

Jordan: THANK YOU. GA

Bravin: OKAY, BYE. SK[2]

---

2. In a TTY conversation, all the type appears in capital letters, "GA" means "go ahead," and "SK" means "stop keying" and the call is ended.

It was a short conversation considering the magnitude of the event. Inside, I was an emotional wreck, but I had to show that I was in control of the situation. King later told me that he felt I was unusually curt, considering we had met during the interviews. I was obviously affected by the turn of events.

Next, Lil Holt called the PR staff on campus to tell them to distribute the press release announcing Zinser's selection and to destroy the other two piles of releases. Subsequently, Jane and I were interviewed together by various reporters from local radio stations, TV stations, and newspapers. I emphasize the word *together* here because Jane wanted me included as a member of the deaf community. At that time, I appreciated the gesture, just as I respected her for asking me to run the search. During one of those interviews, she mentioned the vote was not unanimous. I had never intended to reveal this information, but she gave me an opening to reveal the actual vote down the road, if it became necessary.

Soon after Jane and I completed the interviews, we received word from Gallaudet security that the campus was "in flames." The people on campus had set fire to copies of the press release and were now marching in groups toward some unknown destination. I later learned that they were miffed for two reasons—first because Zinser was not deaf, and second because the announcement was made on a piece of paper rather than in person. Within a short time, we were told that people had started congregating outside the Mayflower. We had kept our location a secret, but, obviously, the news had leaked out. The crowd started to get bigger, and when I looked out the window, I recognized some faces—not just students, but faculty, staff, and local alumni as well.

Lil came to me on the verge of tears. We hugged each other, and she signed, "All the hard work has to end up like this." I responded by saying, "Yes, true, but we stuck to what we needed to do, finding a pool of candidates for the board to decide, and we did good. The rest is up to the board." We hugged again.

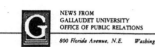

NEWS FROM
GALLAUDET UNIVERSITY
OFFICE OF PUBLIC RELATIONS

800 Florida Avenue, N.E.   Washington, D.C. 20002   (202) 651-5505

3-6-88
(2 pages)

FOR IMMEDIATE RELEASE
March 6, 1988

CONTACT: Barbara H. Dennis
          Chris Beakey
          (202) 651-5505

GALLAUDET UNIVERSITY APPOINTS FIRST WOMAN PRESIDENT

WASHINGTON, D.C. — The Board of Trustees of Gallaudet University has selected
Elisabeth Ann Zinser, Ph.D., vice chancellor for academic affairs at the University of
North Carolina, as Gallaudet University's new president. She is the first woman to be
selected president in the school's 124-year history.

Zinser, 48, will become Gallaudet's seventh president since it was founded in
1864; she replaces Dr. Jerry C. Lee whose tenure as president began in May 1984.
Lee's resignation became effective December 31, 1987.

"Dr. Elizabeth Zinser is a top caliber academician who brings to the office of
president both comprehensive administrative skills and a breadth of experience and
expertise in higher education," said Jane Bassett Spilman, chairman of the Gallaudet
University Board of Trustees. "She is a humanitarian with a deep sense of commitment
and caring — qualities which are essential at a special institution such as
Gallaudet. The Board of Trustees is confident that Dr. Elizabeth Zinser will prove to
be an effective and innovative leader who will represent Gallaudet University with
distinction."

Zinser was selected following a pervasive six month search by a 10-member
committee comprised of board members, key representatives of the faculty, staff,
administration, student body and alumni. Philip Bravin, chairman of the Presidential
Search Committee and a Gallaudet graduate, said, "As chair of the Search Committee, I
am pleased that my committee has been able to respond to the charge given to us by the
Board. This process has been a long and rewarding one and on behalf of the committee,
I wish Dr. Zinser the best in this new assignment."

—more—

The press release announcing Zinser's selection. Courtesy of the
author's personal files.

I knew she was working hard behind the scenes with the police
officers and with the board to make sure we all were taken care
of, and I wondered to myself what would happen next.

Lil had made arrangements for the board to have dinner
in the hotel, so we all went into a private dining room. The
purpose of the dinner was to welcome Larry Speakes, the
former press secretary to President Ronald Reagan, as a new
board member. Larry was very sociable and appeared not to be

perturbed by the protesters who were gathered outside right below the dining room. I figured he must be used to it, knowing how often protesters appeared outside the White House gates during the 1980s.

While trying to eat my shrimp cocktail appetizer, I was constantly interrupted by hotel staff, reporters outside the dining room who were asking to talk to me, and other board members who were looking out the window at the protesters and the DC police. A police sergeant asked to meet with Jane, and she pulled me aside to go with her to meet with the officer. The sergeant spoke to us very authoritatively and unemotionally through an ASL interpreter. She related that sometimes in a protest like this, the most effective way to defuse such a situation is to meet with the protesters. At first, I did not think it was necessary because any meeting would not change the decision, but the sergeant insisted that it might help prevent the situation from getting out of hand. So, Jane and I agreed to the meeting.

We asked that a select group of protesters be chosen and to keep the number small so that a productive discussion could take place. Then we had to find a place where the board representatives could meet with the student and community representatives. Jane and I asked Thomas Penfield Jackson to be the other board representative, and Gustave Rathe asked to be included, so we made him part of the group. We felt the presence of a federal judge would help legitimize the situation and show the seriousness of the situation from our side.

The hotel found a room where we and the protesters could meet, and the staff set up the chairs in such a way that Jane, Gustave, Thomas, and I would sit facing a row of chairs for the student and community representatives. The interpreters would be positioned on the side so that everyone at the meeting would have a clear line of sight. The deaf representatives were Timothy Rarus, the former president of the SBG at Gallaudet; Greg Hlibok, the current president of the SBG; and Jeff Rosen, a deaf lawyer and Gallaudet graduate. I knew all of them very well. Timothy served on the PSC and, as I mentioned earlier, I had known him since he was a baby; Greg went to school with my children, and my wife and I socialized with his parents often in New York; Jeff's mother, Roz Rosen, was an administrator at Gallaudet, and we had grown up in the same neighborhood in New York.

The meeting started around 8 p.m. with Jane explaining the board's position and how well qualified Elisabeth Zinser was for the job. She expressed confidence that Zinser would do the job well and would learn ASL and be up to speed in short order. She would be starting July 1st. This did not sit very well with the three deaf representatives, who constantly bombarded Jane with questions and comments. The back and forth became quite heated at times, and after one of Jeff's questions, Jane purportedly uttered, "Deaf people are not able to function in a hearing world." Jeff quickly shot back, "Did you say what you just said—deaf people are not able to function in a hearing world?" I saw Jane's utterance through an interpreter, as did the other deaf people in the room. Jane quickly responded, "No, I didn't mean what I said, I meant . . ." At that point, all was lost; the room became noisy, and the representatives stormed out. To be fair to everyone, the room was loud, and the acoustics were not the best. I asked both of the interpreters afterward if they had trouble hearing, and their answer was yes. I don't recall asking Gustave or Thomas to verify what Jane had said, as the situation quickly was beyond repair, and nothing they could say would have helped.

Instead of defusing the situation, as the police officers had suggested, Jane's apparent remark inflamed the protesters and became the battle cry for the rest of the DPN movement. Jane was visibly shaken after this. I comforted her for being shaken up but, at the same time, was personally surprised that she possibly made such a statement. I knew her pretty well, and we had developed a close relationship during the search process. She also had appointed me to chair the management review committee

for Dr. Lee back in 1984. It was hard for me to reconcile the trust she had placed in me with the statement she allegedly made in the meeting. It bordered on disbelief. One of the interpreters said Jane could have used a double negative, so, giving her the benefit of the doubt, there could have been a misinterpretation, especially considering the poor acoustics in the room. However, it was a done deal—this was not a repairable situation.

I went back into the private room to eat my shrimp cocktail, but Jane, Gustave, and Thomas pulled me aside to suggest that we make an effort to meet with the crowd outside the Mayflower. DC police assured us that they would be around for our safety and continued to believe that by talking to the protesters, we could still defuse the situation. After Jane's earlier statement, I wasn't sure if it would help, but I went along anyway.

The four of us and an ASL interpreter went outside to address the crowd. We were greeted by the noisy crowd signing and screaming "Deaf President Now!" As I looked around, one deaf guy I knew very well waved to get my attention and signed to me, "Phil—you Judas!" This shattered me emotionally to the core, but I maintained my composure; internally, I was a wreck. After all, I was a true-blooded member of the deaf community—I had deaf parents, a deaf sister, a deaf wife, and three deaf children. My wife had deaf parents and grandparents on both sides and three deaf siblings. To be called a *traitor* was a shock to my system.

Jane began talking to the protesters using the party line she uttered in the room during the meeting with the representatives. The crowd was annoyed and impatient, not hearing anything new. They already knew about the comment Jane apparently had made. While she was talking, I tried to think of how I could make it clear that I was not a Judas. It then occurred to me that the crowd did not know how the board voted. They must have assumed it was a unanimous vote, which, of course wasn't the case.

I interrupted Jane and asked her if I could speak to the crowd. As I knew she would, she said sure and stepped aside to let me come forward. I stated to the crowd,

> Good evening, everyone. I know exactly how upset you are. As you may know, the board voted **ten to four**; of the four, three were deaf and one was hearing. The deaf people on the board tried to represent you, we tried to make our case, but the majority prevailed in this case. I want you to know that, and that is the way America works. (transcribed from video)

I felt a lot better after making that statement. As soon as I finished, Jane resumed talking and taking questions from the crowd. During the exchanges, Jane made a cultural error

A key moment in front of the Mayflower with Philip Bravin announcing that the vote of the board was ten for Zinser and four for Jordan. Note the sign for ten and four. Note the police protection. Interpreter Janet Bailey is on the right, Jane Spilman is on the left, and Judge Thomas Jackson is behind Spilman. Courtesy of the Gallaudet University Video Library.

several times by turning to talk to Gustave and Thomas in front of everyone without including me and without using an interpreter. Some people in the crowd noticed this and felt it was condescending, which did not help the sensitive nature of the situation. Jane also told the crowd that the board would be meeting with the campus community at the Field House the next day.

When Jane finished talking, several student and community representatives addressed the crowd and inflamed them with Jane's apparent comment. They then urged the protesters to march to the White House. At that time, I wasn't sure what would happen next. Jane, Gustave, Thomas, and I went back upstairs to the room where the other board members were waiting. We discussed strategies and logistics for the meeting on Monday, and then most of the board members returned to campus for the evening. I needed time to collect my thoughts and emotions, so I asked Jane if I could spend the night at the Mayflower, and she said, "Sure."

By the time I went up to my room, it was close to 11 p.m., so I turned on the news and saw the protest. I wept uncontrollably. After the finalists' interviews and up until the vote, I had confidence that Gallaudet would have a deaf president. I. King Jordan did well in his interview, as did Zinser, but the simple fact was that, all things being equal, it was time for a deaf president. Boards rarely, if ever, change their mind, and I concluded that the next opportunity for a deaf president would be after Zinser's term, which Gallaudet did not deserve. That night, I did not sleep well at all. And the hunger pangs I felt in bed were a reminder of the unfinished shrimp cocktail.

2

Monday, March 7

When I woke up Monday morning at the Mayflower, little did I know what the course going forward would be like. I had a message that someone from Gallaudet would be picking me up, so I got out of bed and went to get the *Washington Post* outside my hotel room. There, on the front page was the headline "Hearing Educator Chosen President of Gallaudet U."[3] (As an aside, looking back, it was interesting to note that the *Washington Post* used the term *hearing educator* as to make a point.) It occurred to me that this was bigger news than we had thought. Usually, the selection of the Gallaudet president appeared on page A15 or even in the Metro section, but the front page! I got dressed and went downstairs to wait outside for a Gallaudet security car to pick me up. Gustave Rathe was already inside the car. The officer told us the students had shut down the campus, and no one was allowed in. After weaving through the morning rush-hour traffic, we arrived at the main gate on Florida Avenue. It was a sight that I did not anticipate—a sea of students, faculty, staff, and community members blocking the main entrance to the campus. I asked the officer to drive around the perimeter of the campus to see whether we could get in through another gate, but he told me that students had sealed the whole perimeter, and there was no other way to get in.

I told the officer to drop me off in front and I would walk on to the campus. The officer cautioned me about my safety under the circumstances, but I felt it was important for me to show my face, even in "defeat," but—in a way—to be one of them. I did not realize what I would be getting into—I didn't

---

3. Molly Sinclair and Karlyn Harker, "Hearing Educator Chosen President of Gallaudet U," *Washington Post*, March 7, 1988.

Phil talking to his son, Jeff, after getting on campus on Monday. Note the reporter following, the TV cameras on the right. Courtesy of the Gallaudet University Archives.

expect any restraint nor physical harm, so I got out of the car and walked into the crowd. The sea "parted" for me, and I felt relieved when I saw a young kid running up to me and hugging me—it was my son Jeff. Jeff asked if I was okay, and I said, "Sure." We chatted a bit and walked together up to the back of Fowler Hall, where a bunch of reporters waited to chase down any possibility of new "news," and I happened to be the one they saw at that moment. I was ready to go over to the Kendall apartments where the rest of the Board was staying, and this was an unplanned moment.

After Jeff and I hugged each other goodbye, the reporters started to interview me. I didn't have an ASL interpreter with me, so I spoke very slowly and carefully, using whoever was able to interpret my signs into voice for the reporters and hoping my message was delivered as correctly as I recited it. There's always a risk in dealing with interpreters you've never worked with. I usually like to chat with them before I do anything in public to be sure they understand my signs, nuances, and New York signing style, which is pretty fast.[4] One of the reporters asked if there was any room for compromise, and I responded, "I am not in a position to comment on that."

After the interview, campus security took me to the Kendall apartments on the other side of the campus. The apartments are on top of Kendall School, which is an elementary school for deaf and hard of hearing children in the Washington, DC, metropolitan area. Whenever the board members came to Gallaudet, they usually stayed at the apartments, which was very convenient. Some board members were already there, and others started to trickle in. Once everyone arrived, we had an informal meeting with Jane to rehash the events of the day before and to think of what we needed to tell the community that afternoon. We all agreed that nothing would need to change as a result of the protest; in other words, we would not be changing our decision, and we would give Dr. Zinser all the support she needed going forward. My thinking at that time was to make the best of the situation— support Dr. Zinser all the way and not think of replacing her at the moment.

During this meeting, we received a request from a representative of a campus group calling themselves "The Group of Seventeen."[5] It was made up of various student, faculty, and

---

4. Yes, there are different signing styles. Anecdotally, New Yorkers sign very fast and move their mouths, and Southern folks sign slowly (akin to a spoken drawl). Midwesterners sign very properly and usually do not move their mouths while signing. There also are regional signs. Signs can differ not only from one region to another, but from one state to another, and even from one school to another in the same state. The signs for "birthday" or "Halloween" are dramatic examples of differences in regional signs.

5. According to the memory of the author, there were seventeen people that showed up. The author did ask members of the community who were there, and their memory of "seventeen" was fuzzy, while mine was clear, and my notes reflected that.

staff representatives. From our point of view, it was hard to assess the legitimacy of such a group, but we agreed to meet with them.

The Group of Seventeen came into the room, and we sat in a large circle so that we could all see each other. I knew practically everyone in the group on a first-name basis. The group presented us with four demands and said the protest would end when the demands were met. The demands were (1) the appointment of a deaf president, (2) Spilman's resignation from the board, (3) a deaf majority (51 percent) on the board of trustees, and (4) no reprisals against the protesters. We acknowledged receiving the demands and asserted that our position would not change. We told the group that Zinser was duly selected and that she would start in the summer. We continued the meeting, but neither side budged. Jane did most of the talking, with some board members adding comments to clarify or buttress her comments. It should be noted that Jane's comments were basically boilerplate: "Zinser was best qualified . . . she will learn sign language . . . the board made its decision, and it is final." She never strayed from those.

One person in the group of protesters suggested that a mediator be brought in to facilitate things, but first, we decided to recess so that each side could discuss possible solutions to the stalemate. The board felt there was not much to move on. Any indication of wavering would give the protesters hope that Zinser's selection could be compromised, and no board would take such an action a day after a protest. When the two groups came back together, the protest representatives suggested that three of their members meet with three board members to see if they could reach a solution, and Jane Spilman agreed to it.

Harvey Goodstein, a faculty member; William Marshall, chair of the President's Council on Deafness and a faculty member; Timothy Rarus represented the Group of Seventeen; and Spilman and two hearing board members represented the board. After this meeting, Spilman said she would talk to the board.

When the full board and the Group of Seventeen reconvened, Spilman introduced Kenneth Wells Parkinson, a Gallaudet attorney.[6] He had recommended that the board not change its decision, and Spilman reported this to the group. She then said it was time to go to the Field House to meet with whoever was assembled there. Personally, I was torn; being a deaf person, I knew how the representatives on the other side felt, and being a board member, I knew the board's position. First and foremost, the board had to maintain control of the situation—not the protest, but the institution of Gallaudet. Any division or split would have long-term consequences. Some people would think otherwise, but having served for many years on various boards has led me to believe that 99 percent of the public does not have a keen understanding of how boards function or their legitimate role in institutions.

At this point, I was trying to assess the situation. The campus was locked down. The students had control of the gates, and they could very well seal us in on campus. I wondered how we were going to get out, and I am sure the same was true of my colleagues on the board.

A campus van picked us up and took us to the back entrance of the Field House. The Field House was familiar territory to us because the board always sat on stage for commencement, a happy annual event. But this was not a happy event, rather one with potential hostility. I turned to my good friend and mentor, Alexander Patterson, in the back room and asked him if we would be okay. Alex, in his reassuring way, said, "Phil, in my

---

6. Kenneth Parkinson had been in Washington a long time. In 1972, he had been counsel to the Committee to Re-elect the President. He was a member of the "Watergate Seven," who were indicted by a federal grand jury on March 1, 1974. For his involvement, he faced a maximum of ten years in prison and $10,000 in fines. Parkinson was acquitted on January 1, 1975. Lesley Oelsner, "Parkinson Denies Knowingly Playing Watergate-Payment Role," *New York Times*, December 19, 1974, https://www.nytimes.com/1974/12/19/archives/parkinson-denies-knowingly-playing-watergatepayment-role-passed-on.html.

Four of the trustees (Frank Sullivan, Robert Sanderson, Laurel Glass, and Phil Bravin) who voted for I. King Jordan on stage in the Gallaudet Field House on Monday. The fifth trustee on the far right is Jean Crabtree. Courtesy of the Gallaudet University Video Library.

professional life in the past, I was once airlifted by a helicopter out of a coup in Kenya, and look at me today. This cannot be any worse. We will be okay." I literally rolled my eyes, but I had so much faith in the guy that I took him at his word and went into the Field House with the rest of the board.

Once we were assembled on the stage, I looked out at the angry group filling the floor seats and bleachers. I recognized many of the faces in the crowd, so I was careful not to sign to my deaf colleagues, since deaf people can read sign language from a distance. I didn't sign to my hearing colleagues through an interpreter either, for the same reason. I didn't want to send the wrong signal to the audience. Jane stood up and went to the podium as our designated leader. As soon as she started speaking, there were shouts from the group. She read from a scripted message—almost the same one she gave to the Group of Seventeen before we left Kendall School. Then, I went to the podium to give a short statement. My hidden agenda was to say something for the deaf members of the board, to let the protesters know that we had not supported Zinser. I told the crowd, "This was all we could do; we did our best."

Jane got up to speak again, but some in the crowd were yelling and signing at her. When she said she couldn't hear what people were saying, one member of the audience shouted, "Well, you never learned sign language." At that moment, I realized the situation was deteriorating and that dialogue was not happening; instead, the schism was widening, and the audience was angry. I knew very well that meaningful dialogue can't happen when one party is angry—anger overcomes any attempt to reason. Not long after this, someone pulled the fire alarm, and the alarm bell lights started flashing. (This, in a way, rendered communication useless because the hearing board members and Jane could not hear the voice of the interpreters—or whoever came on stage—due to the noise of the alarms.) A few minutes later (it felt longer than that), Harvey Goodstein, a deaf faculty member who I grew up with in New York, walked up to the stage next to Jane and said that a group had met with the board and that the board did not agree to the demands. He asked of the audience, "Why not leave?" This was a stunner— we watched as the sea of people drained out almost immediately; only a few people remained in the huge Field House. At that point, I felt the electricity leave the room. People had come to ask questions, and questions had been answered; but it was a fruitless exercise, one to satisfy only those who asked, and they weren't listening because they knew the answers anyway.

After answering more questions and hearing comments from the remaining people, Jane called an end to the meeting. She then told us we could leave campus. I learned later that after Harvey Goodstein convinced most of the audience to leave, everyone went down to the Florida Avenue gate to get ready to march to the Capitol.

A dramatic and iconic picture of Harvey Goodstein interrupting Jane Spilman in the Gallaudet Field House on Monday. Courtesy of the Gallaudet University Video Library.

When the group was down at the gate, it was blocked by the DC police; a DC police officer said they couldn't march without a permit. At that point, Gary Olsen, the executive director of the National Association of the Deaf and one of the primary movers of the events leading up to and during the protest, went to the police officer in charge and offered to interpret for him. The officer welcomed the opportunity. Gary climbed up on a platform, so everyone could see him and asked the officer what message he wanted to relay. When the officer said, "Please tell them they cannot march or walk in a group off-campus without a permit," Gary started to sign, but unbeknownst to the officer, who didn't understand ASL anyway, Gary signed, "Ignore what the officer says. Let's go ahead and march to the Capitol."

Lo and behold, everyone walked out onto Florida Avenue. The officers could not physically control the mass, so they ran to their cars and brought out their bullhorns, not realizing they would be useless in this crowd. They had lost control of the situation, so instead, they ended up following the protesters to the Capitol. I had anticipated and mentioned the possibility of this loss of control in my meeting with Gallaudet security several days before. But when I said the DC police force could use some training, my suggestion was shot down.

Ironically, the march off campus orchestrated by Harvey Goodstein and Gary Olsen (who, incidentally were roommates at Gallaudet for most of their undergraduate years and whom I knew very well) gave me and the other board members the opportunity to leave campus without the potential of being blocked by the protesters. Drivers provided by the university's Department of Transportation picked up our bags at the apartments and came to get us at the Field House to take us to the various airports serving the DC area. I went back to the apartment to collect some things and then walked across campus to the transportation garage only to find that everyone had already left. My bags were in one of those vehicles, so I had to stay in the garage for a couple of hours and wait for the vans to come back. When they finally did, I got my bags, and someone drove me to National (Reagan) Airport for my flight home.

During the flight, I reflected on what had happened over the past two days. We had not reached any resolution with the protesters, and we had left campus in a huff, without a plan. Jane Spilman stayed behind to deal with the problem. This might seem unusual, but it is normal for a chair to represent the board in public between meetings. This is usually true of most of the boards in the country. Our final advice to Jane was to stick by our decision to make Zinser the next president of Gallaudet, and she dutifully did that for the next few days. This was not a sign of "abandonment" by the board. Rather, because there was no alternative to our decision, there was nothing different Jane could do except to maintain that position. Any change in stance would of course require that the board meet again.

"Hearing Educator Chosen President of Gallaudet U." Front page of the *Washington Post* on March 7, 1988. From The Washington Post. © 1988 The Washington Post. All rights reserved. Used under license. http://www.washingtonpost.com.

3

Tuesday, March 8

On Tuesday morning, I opened the *New York Times* and found a photograph of the Gallaudet protesters on the front page. The caption read, "Protest Over Choice of President Shuts College for the Deaf."[7] The story inside on page A20 noted that Spilman described Zinser as a "caring" person. To a person outside the deaf community, the use of the word *caring* may seem innocuous. To a deaf person, however, it can be interpreted as patronizing, and it intimates that we need hearing people to take care of us. The deaf community prides itself on being self-sufficient. We coexist, work, and live with hearing people as equals, not as second-class citizens.

During the day on Tuesday, the board members kept calling each other. We hadn't heard from Jane Spilman and, therefore, didn't know what was going on in Washington. Most of what we knew came from newspaper reports. However, we sensed that not all of this was necessarily firsthand information, so we were somewhat in the dark. Even Lil Holt, who was working out of the Transportation Department on campus, didn't know what was really going on. Legally, nothing had changed. According to the press accounts coming in, it seemed that Jane was still in DC, dealing indirectly with the protesters via some third party. After some phone calls, we learned (independently of Jane), that she had retained a public relations firm to deal with the issue. The message was basically, "Nothing's changed—Zinser

---

7. Lena Williams, "College for the Deaf Is Shut by Protest Over President," *New York Times*, March 8, 1988.

is still president," but the campus was closed down, and the protesters kept rallying—burning Zinser in effigy, for one thing. Jane's retention of such a firm was necessary. It was within her responsibilities as chair. Whether she checked with other members of the board on this action, I have no knowledge nor documentation.

I decided to make more calls from my IBM office in White Plains, NY. Remember in those days, making a phone call was cumbersome for deaf people. We had to use a relay service, and the speed of conversation was based on how fast one typed. I called Lil Holt again and learned she found out where Jane was and how I could reach her. I also learned that afternoon that the Gallaudet University Alumni Association president announced that the alumni board voted to support the students and their four demands. They also contributed $1,000 to the cause.

By Tuesday evening, the protest had become a media event—TV trucks converged on campus, and Gallaudet made the national evening news on television. Peter Jennings, the ABC TV anchor, was on top of the protest, and he made this the lead story on the news that night. I had a conversation with Alexander Patterson by phone and, after some discussion, he told me to "go down to DC and find out what's going on and get back to us if Jane can't."

"Students Close Gallaudet U." Front page of the *Washington Post* on March 8, 1988. From The Washington Post. © 1988 The Washington Post. All rights reserved. Used under license. http://www.washingtonpost.com.

4

Wednesday, March 9

On Wednesday, I stayed home to make some calls before going into work. I finally connected with Jane at the public relations firm, Peabody Fitzpatrick, on K Street in downtown DC. During this call, Jane suggested that I come down to meet with her and others (I didn't know who the others were). Soon after, I received some blistering phone calls from some of the members of the newly formed Deaf President Now Council (which was partially made up of the original Group of Seventeen), people I had known and been friends with for a long time. They felt the deaf members of the board—myself, Robert Sanderson, and Frank Sullivan—ought to resign en masse in protest.

I was typing all morning on the TTY, with my legs shaking due to the emotional and confrontational nature of some of the calls. I had rarely encountered such calls in my life and was not used to dealing with them.

I called Robert and Frank, and we collectively agreed not to resign for the simple reason that if we did, there would be no deaf voice on the board, and there would be no way for us to be reelected if things changed. Once we resigned, we would be powerless to make things happen, simple as that. In later conversations with deaf callers, I told them that we weren't resigning for the reasons I just outlined. They did not like this response, as they were adamant on us resigning, but that was the end of the discussion. In hindsight, not resigning was a key action, considering what took place the following Sunday.

I finished all my calls and then got ready to drive to LaGuardia Airport, which was only twenty-five minutes from my home. In 1988, two airlines provided shuttle service to DC—one did it every hour on the hour, and the other every hour on the half hour. No matter when I got to the airport, I didn't have to wait long for a plane. No security checkpoints existed then, so it was a mere fifteen minutes from my car to the ticket counter and to the gate. When I arrived in DC in the early afternoon, I took a cab to the offices of Peabody Fitzpatrick Communications. I knew Gallaudet had used this firm in the past, but I didn't know anyone there. A receptionist greeted me as soon as I walked in and whisked me into a meeting room. Upon entering the room, I was very surprised to see Elisabeth Zinser at the head of the table. Then, I saw Jane, Kenneth Wells Parkinson, the Gallaudet attorney; Catherine Ingold, the provost; Jim Barnes, the vice president of Business and Administration; two ASL interpreters; and two women I did not know. I soon found out that they were the principals of the firm, Myra Peabody and Joyce Fitzpatrick. I noticed right away that there were no other deaf people in the room, which made me very angry. I asked Jane what the people in the room were doing. She replied that "they were discussing strategies and alternatives to deal with the mushrooming protest that was happening on campus."

I was furious and responded, "How can you do this if there are no deaf people in the room?" I could see everyone's eyes widen in surprise. For those who know me, I rarely display anger in public, but this situation was unconscionable—here was a group of hearing people who had no association with deaf culture discussing how to deal with deaf people. I asked why Elisabeth was in the room, since we had agreed at the board meeting on Sunday that she would not start until July 1st. Jane pointed to Kenneth, who said that it was all legitimate; however, this action had been taken without the board's input. I expressed my doubts to Jane, Elisabeth, and Kenneth about the legitimacy of Zinser's role without a formal board resolution. Jane turned to Catherine Ingold and asked her to call in Robert Davila and Mervin Garretson, both of whom were deaf and were on the Central Administration Management Team

(CAMT) that was running Gallaudet (Ingold and Barnes also were on the CAMT).

Even though Davila and Garretson hadn't arrived yet, the discussion turned to strategies for a meeting that was to take place at 4:00 that afternoon with Congressmen David Bonior (D-MI) and Steve Gunderson (R-WI). The Gallaudet University Board of Trustees, by federal law, has three congressional members (two from the House and one from the Senate). Bonior and Gunderson were the House representatives, and Daniel Inouye (D-HI) was the Senate representative. Senator Inouye rarely attended board meetings, but Bonior and Gunderson came from time to time, despite their busy schedules. They both took Gallaudet to heart.

In deliberating what to tell Bonior and Gunderson, the group meeting at Peabody Fitzpatrick took the position that nothing would change. Zinser was the new and duly appointed president (according to Jane Spilman and Kenneth Parkinson), and that would be the message delivered to Bonior and Gunderson. Privately, my position *had* changed, especially after what I had seen earlier at the Peabody Fitzpatrick office. Something just didn't smell right, and the fact that deaf people were excluded from that meeting—intentionally or unintentionally—did not sit right with me. I began to harbor doubts about Spilman and Zinser. They should have known better. This, for me, was the turning point in my support of them. I also had read an article in the *Washington Post* that morning, quoting Bonior as saying that congressional leaders were concerned about the Gallaudet situation and that the college's funding could be in jeopardy.[8] I suspected Bonior would be articulating the congressional concern at the meeting.

When it was time to go to Capitol Hill, Zinser, Spilman, and I, along with the interpreters, took a taxi over to the House

---

8. Molly Sinclair and Eric Pianin, "Protest May Imperil Gallaudet Funding," *Washington Post*, March 9, 1988.

Office Building. We met in Congressman Bonior's office, where he had a round table. Congressman Gunderson came in a few minutes later. Both congressmen expressed their concern about what was happening at Gallaudet. Before the meeting started, Bonior asked his staff to leave (this was an unusual gesture). Bonior also told us to leave through a side door after the meeting since the press was waiting in front of the main entrance to his office. Both congressmen talked about the threat to Gallaudet of losing federal funding if the protest and the closure of campus continued for a long time. They also told us that earlier that day, they met with members of the Gallaudet community, who thought Zinser was not qualified to be president.

The discussion at the round table was interesting. Both Bonior and Gunderson came close to asking Zinser and Spilman to reconsider. They were not very specific as to what action ought to be taken, but the message was definitely clear—Zinser ought to resign. I was there primarily as an observer and to help fill in some of the factual gaps, especially as they related to the search. The congressmen were not quite aware that there had been six semifinalists, three of whom were deaf. They were not present at the meeting when Zinser was selected. The meeting went on for close to an hour and, at the end, no progress had been made. Both Spilman and Zinser stood their ground.

In the back of my mind, I wondered if the other board members still supported their original decision, considering the events of the past few days. They obviously didn't know what had transpired earlier that afternoon. Frank Sullivan was in town, and he had accompanied Jane to some of the public meetings, but he was not present in the conference room at Peabody Fitzpatrick.

After the meeting, I asked to speak privately with Bonior (Gunderson had already left). While Spilman and Zinser waited outside the room, I told Bonior that I thought they were not reading the situation correctly, and he agreed. I also told him that Jane had not been in communication with the board and that we were being left in the dark, learning information in bits and pieces from the press and the community. He made the comment that as a member of Congress, there is a pulse reading of the seriousness of any matter before Congress. This is dictated by how many members talk among each other about a specific issue. If one or two members speak about something, then he would usually ignore that. But if it came to 25–50 members talking about a matter—then, of course, that would be something he would need to get his hands on—and that was the pulse of Congress that day—at least 50 members were talking about the Gallaudet protest. And, as a result, it was becoming a serious matter for them to pursue. I assured Bonior that I would stay on top of that and communicate with him as needed.[9] We hugged and shook hands, and I went back to the Peabody Fitzpatrick offices with Spilman and Zinser. While Bonior and Gunderson did not participate in the search process, as members of the board, they received periodic updates as other members of the board did.

Back at the office, I was surprised and glad to see Robert Davila. He told us that Mervin Garretson couldn't make it because he was out of town. We debriefed Bob on our discussion with the congressmen, and then we talked about the various options for resolving the protest. Even though the protesters included students, alumni, faculty, staff, and community members, the discussion focused on the students. One of the suggestions was to arrest the protesters, but Bob and I cautioned against this because there had not been much dialogue with them up to this point. It was getting late, and I had intended to

---

9. Twenty years later, I ran into Congressman Bonior in New Hampshire when he was the campaign manager for John Edwards in the Democratic race for the 2008 presidential nomination. It was refreshing to see him again after all those years, and to my amazement, he remembered some ASL and greeted me with a perfect "How are you?" in sign language! Like Congressman Gunderson, he took his task as a Gallaudet trustee seriously, to the point of learning ASL.

go home, so I said my goodbyes and left for the airport before we reached any real decision. I made it to the airport in the nick of time to catch the 9:30 shuttle to New York, which was the last flight of the night. Soon after, the plane was about to take off and aborted while on the runway; the stewardess told me that there was an engine malfunction and we had to return to the gate. Luckily, they found us another plane, and we took off just before the 10 p.m. noise curfew. On the ride home, I decided that I had to renounce my support for Jane. The events of the day, especially at the conference room at Peabody Fitzpatrick, led me to believe the situation was deteriorating and that she and the PR firm were making statements and dealing with the situation in a vacuum. The insensitivity toward and ignorance about deaf people, which took place that afternoon, led me to wonder whether the events of the previous few weeks occurred without my realizing that Jane and other board members were predisposed to choosing a hearing person as president.

When I got home, Judy told me that *Nightline*, a late-night news program on ABC, was going to cover the Gallaudet protest that night. We tuned in and saw Elisabeth Zinser, Greg Hlibok, and Marlee Matlin (a deaf actress and activist) being interviewed by Ted Koppel, the host of the program. The discussion was quite contentious. Hlibok explained the four demands and said that the protesters would not compromise because the time had come for Gallaudet to have a deaf president. In response, Zinser said she had the support of the board, and she was determined to stay until they asked her to resign. Koppel suggested that Zinser acted as if she was a "puppet" of the board and that she could resign if she wanted to. She replied that she had not talked to enough of the people involved to make that decision. After that, the show devolved into chaos, with all three guests talking over each other. To make matters more confusing, Matlin had a male voice interpreter and Hlibok had a female voice interpreter.

For a protest on the campus of a small college to reach the front page of the *Washington Post*, the *New York Times*, the ABC *Evening News*, and *Nightline* spoke of the effective and viral outreach garnered by the protesters and their supporters around the country. I said to myself that evening that something had to give, and that something would be a change of heart from Zinser. I knew for a fact that the board would not budge. Why would it after a ten to four decision? If we changed our decision, it would set a precedent not only for Gallaudet but also for many boards at other colleges and universities. We had gone through a process, respected the process, and dealt with the decision; there was no going back. I came to this conclusion without knowing the other events of the day—that Zinser had met with I. King Jordan, and there had been a press conference at the National Press Club where Jordan announced his support for Zinser—because I had been in meetings and missed the evening news. I didn't find this out until Thursday morning.

"Protest May Imperil Gallaudet Funding." Front page of the *Washington Post* on March 9, 1988. From The Washington Post. © 1988 The Washington Post. All rights reserved. Used under license. http://www.washingtonpost.com.

5

Thursday, March 10

Thursday morning, the *New York Times* ran a story with the headline, "Many in Faculty Back Protest by Deaf."[10] I was ready to go to work that morning, but one phone call after another ensued, so I dropped the idea and stayed home to handle them. In the course of the phone calls, it was confirmed further that the faculty had voted on Wednesday 147 to 5 to support the students' four demands.[11] Also, the grapevine over the phone was abuzz about a news conference that afternoon.

At lunchtime, I was still on the phone. Most of the calls were from board members and from some of the deaf faculty and staff protesters. The deaf faculty and staff who were part of the DPN council again asked me, Robert Sanderson, and Frank Sullivan to resign under protest as a group. I called them both, and we stuck to our decision not to resign for fear of losing the deaf voice on the board (in hindsight, this was a key determination). Instead, we told the council that we would put out a statement expressing our concern about the situation.

The three of us worked out a statement to send to the council, which did not amount to much. We were mindful of staying unified with the rest of the board. Any crack that would be detected in our "armor" would cause the movement to be inflamed again. The council requested that this statement be sent down by FedEx so that no one could leak an unauthorized

10. Drummond Ayres Jr., "Many in Faculty Back Protest by Deaf," *New York Times*, March 10, 1988.

11. The faculty vote has been reported differently in several publications. (I chose to use the one that was given to me over the phone by a source I cannot recall.) In a typical university, if the faculty collectively does not support the administrator in question, this is usually a "fatal" blow to the person's standing at the university.

version, so I drove it over to a FedEx office. To this day, I doubt if this got anywhere or was ever used or opened. No one was able to verify receiving it.

After this, I decided to call Jane to tell her I was upset with the way things were going. I do not recall how I made the call, but it went something like this: After some pleasantries, I told her, "I want to thank you for representing the board this week. I know this was no easy task for you. However, because of what I witnessed at the Peabody Fitzpatrick office yesterday and at the meeting with the congressmen, I have to tell you before I share this with others that I am withdrawing my support for you and Dr. Zinser. I am not sure yet how I will share this information."

Jane then responded by saying, "I am very disappointed, and I hope you will think more about this. This is a difficult time for Gallaudet." And the call ended just like that. I felt a weight come off my shoulders, but I still had to think of a way to announce my decision. I wondered if it would inflame things more, or if it would help move Dr. Zinser. I had always had a strong tendency to count to 100 before doing anything, and this time was no exception. As it turned out, I never had to announce my decision. I received a phone call late Thursday night from a Gallaudet staff person who told me that Elisabeth Zinser had resigned. I was then asked to stand by for further instructions.

The resignation was the break needed to change things and move the situation forward. The board probably would not have budged unless the protesters had done something dramatic and drastic. As it was, spring break started that weekend, and most of the students had plans to leave campus.

I knew the next day would be important. The protesters had a permit to march to the Capitol and rally for a deaf president, and people were coming in from all over the country. I felt it was the students' and the community's day in the spotlight, and I did not want to do anything to take that away from them. I decided to stay in New York.

"Congressman Urges Zinser to Resign." Front page of the *Washington Post* on March 10, 1988. From The Washington Post. © 1988 The Washington Post. All rights reserved. Used under license. http://www.washingtonpost.com.

6

Friday, March 11

This was a very unusual and difficult day for me as a deaf person. Practically every deaf person in America was focused on the national rally for a deaf president in Washington, DC. It also hit home for me because my father, my sister, and my son participated in the march. My mom would have also attended, if not for her bad knees. In my heart, I would have loved to march, but I believed that my responsibilities as a board member dictated otherwise. My participation would not have helped the cause of the movement. It was their day in the sun, not the board's. Furthermore, Jane did not make an effort to contact any of us; we were working through Lil and other Gallaudet staff members.

I was working in my office at IBM in White Plains, NY, when I received a call from Lil Holt telling me that the board would meet on Sunday at the Embassy Row Hotel in DC. She also said that I should check into the hotel as a member of the "Apollo Group." This was an attempt to hide ourselves from the press, which had been on very high alert all week covering the protest.

I called some other board members about the forthcoming meeting, but there was very little new information to share other than that we had to deal with a university without a president. We speculated about how Jane would deal with this whole thing. Elisabeth Zinser had gone back to Greensboro and was now completely out of the picture.

I went home after work that day and watched the coverage of the national rally at the US Capitol on the evening news. I was heartbroken at having missed the rally. At the same time, I was proud that the DPN protest had become the deaf civil

The four student leaders—Tim Rarus, Bridgetta Bourne-Firl, Greg Hlibok, and Jerry Covell—on their way to the Capitol. The sign behind them "The Board Busters" was created by the students. Courtesy of the Gallaudet University Archives.

"We Still Have a Dream" banner. This banner, loaned to the protestors from the Crispus Attucks museum, was used by the students marching to the Capitol on Friday. Courtesy of the Gallaudet University Archives.

rights movement. Nothing symbolized that more clearly than the marchers' use of the "We Still Have a Dream" banner (on loan from the Crispus Attucks Museum) carried by civil rights leaders in their effort to create Martin Luther King Jr. Day.[12, 13] This sent a powerful message to the mainstream media.

12. Jack R. Gannon, *The Week the World Heard Gallaudet* (Washington, DC: Gallaudet University Press, 1989), 109.

13. The Crispus Attucks Museum, once located in Washington, DC, is now in Indianapolis, IN.

"Zinser Quits Gallaudet Amid Student Uproar." Front page of the *Washington Post* on March 11, 1988. From The Washington Post. © 1988 The Washington Post. All rights reserved. Used under license. http://www.washingtonpost.com.

7

Saturday, March 12

Flying down to Washington on Saturday was a surreal experience. Gallaudet had no president, and the chair of the board was silent. I had never experienced a situation like this as a board member. The person we had selected to be the next president had resigned, and no one really was running Gallaudet, except for the board and the CAMT. Actually, at this point, the board was in the dark; only Jane knew what was going on, and the nation was watching every move we made. That morning, the *New York Times* ran a story on the front page with the headline "Demonstrations by the Deaf Bring a Resignation but Not Yet a Truce."[14] The article reported that the protesters intended to keep the university closed until the board selected a deaf president. I wondered how the board members would react when we all got together on Sunday.

After arriving at the airport, I took a cab to the Embassy Row Hotel and checked in as a member of the Apollo Group.[15] I saw some other board members in the lobby, and we agreed to have dinner together. The interpreters also were there, so there was full communication between the deaf and hearing members. Normally, when the interpreters were not around, communication between us was limited and superficial. Sometimes, Frank Sullivan would speak for the deaf members, but when hearing people spoke to us, it was a guessing game because lipreading is rarely more than 25 percent accurate.

---

14. Drummond R. Ayres, "Demonstrations by the Deaf Bring a Resignation but Not Yet a Truce," *New York Times*, March 12, 1988.

15. This "disguise" didn't work. The press was stationed outside the hotel with satellite trucks and reporters standing by.

Over dinner, we talked about how things had turned around the past week and how we basically were shut off from Jane. Except for my trip to DC on Wednesday, none of us had heard from her. Our discussion then turned to what the next steps should be. Common sense would dictate that the first order of business would be to select a leader to run Gallaudet, either for the interim or permanently. We also speculated as to how Jane would handle the whole thing, whether she would step down as board chair or even from the board, or remain on the board. No one had a good reading of what Jane would do, considering she had a rough week. I am of the opinion (with the benefit of hindsight) that more communication could have taken place during that week, but then any decision during the week would naturally require board consensus. What I do not know is whether the executive committee was consulted during that week, but I know for a fact that there was no formal meeting of the executive committee that week, as there are no minutes reflecting such meetings.

"Students Hail Zinser Resignation." Front page of the *Washington Post* on March 12, 1988. From The Washington Post. © 1988 The Washington Post. All rights reserved. Used under license. http://www.washingtonpost.com.

8

Sunday, March 13

At 10:00 a.m. Sunday morning, the board gathered in the Continental Room on one of the lower levels of the hotel. This location was chosen purposely to avoid prying eyes and ears. Jane presided at the meeting, and all the board members except for Senator Inouye and Laurel Glass, who was ill, were in attendance. Even the new trustee, Larry Speakes, and Congressmen Bonior and Gunderson were present, as were Robert Davila, Jim Barnes, and Catherine Ingold from the CAMT; Kenneth Parkinson; ASL interpreters; and the ever-faithful Lil Holt. (Merv Garretson was still out of town.)

The mood in the room was somber, which wasn't surprising considering the events of the previous week and what we needed to deal with going forward. The meeting began with a presentation by the members of the CAMT on how the university would need to resume operations after they consulted with the Council of Deans, the directors of Business and Administration, and the university and precollege programs faculty leaders.[16]

The collective recommendations were as follows:

- Establish a moratorium on the protest between the board of trustees and the DPN Council to allow normal operations of the university.
- Schedule a meeting between the board of trustees and the DPN council to discuss the remaining demands.
- Appoint a new president and, if necessary, appoint an interim president.
- Report through the CAMT to keep the campus informed.

---

16. The following description of the meeting is based on excerpts and my paraphrasing from the actual minutes of the meeting, as well as the addition of my personal observations.

In addition, the CAMT presented a plan to maintain stability in the administrative positions at the university to deal with the forthcoming budget hearings in Congress. They also recommended no administrative changes at the university for the next six months to ensure business as usual and establish stability on campus. The board thanked the CAMT for the information and then asked them to leave the room. The board then went into executive session.

After much discussion on the sanctions and amnesty demands the protesters had made, the board decided on a set of rules to be presented to the new president and the campus community regarding reprisals and future actions. There were some board members with legal, public relations, and political backgrounds. They all contributed in different ways. Also, the deaf board members had the community point of view. Under normal circumstances, the events of the previous week would not be tolerated at all by any board, but we agreed that the week had been an aberration. In fact, we considered it a social and civil rights movement. However, we also decided that no such actions would be tolerated in the future. The rules were incorporated in the following statement:

1. No sanctions shall be imposed on university students, administrators, faculty, or employees who participated in the protest or those who didn't. All rights of students and employees shall be protected.
2. Any university employee who fails to carry out their responsibilities in a satisfactory manner shall be subject to disciplinary action up to and including dismissal from the university.
3. Any individual who interferes with the normal operations of the university will be subject not only to the regulations of the university but also to the laws of the District of Columbia and the United States of America.
4. All regulations of the university will be enforced.

Coming to agreement on the statement took a lot of soul searching and some legal and political considerations (e.g., the reaction from the deaf community), especially with the Gallaudet attorney, the congressmen, and the former presidential press secretary there. Many of the board members did not like the perception that we had lost control of the institution, so calling the protest a social and civil rights movement was a concession. Maintaining control and not letting this happen again was a major thrust of the statement.

After we finished the statement, we took a break. When we reconvened, we formally accepted Zinser's resignation. Jane then asked Kenneth Parkinson to review the bylaws of the board and lay out the options for selecting the eighth president of Gallaudet. First, he told us the search process for the seventh president had been conducted correctly and there were no flaws in the selection process. Then, he explained that the bylaws of the board give the board ultimate authority to appoint the president of the university. Lastly, he said that the board could choose the next president from among the remaining candidates, add to the candidates, start the search process over, or select an acting, interim, or a permanent president.

After exploring all our options, we decided that we and the university needed closure of the whole matter, so to go forward, we had to select a permanent president. If a new search was to take place or an interim president selected, some of the remnants of the past week could be repeated. To avoid reopening the emotions of the past week, and to start "clean" and move forward, the board agreed to appoint Dr. I. King Jordan as the next president of Gallaudet University. While the initial vote was not unanimous, a motion was made to make it unanimous, and it carried.

Then came the stunner. Jane Spilman offered her resignation as chair and from the board effective immediately. She said the events of the past week had taken a lot out of her personally and felt that new leadership was needed going forward.

The room went silent for some time. Some of us had antic-ipated her resignation as chair, but resigning from the board was a complete surprise. After some very nice and heartfelt responses from the attendees, the board reluctantly accepted her resignation with much appreciation for her service and, at the same time, with deep regret. She then left the room after some hugs and words of comfort from many of the trustees.

The next order of business then became the selection of the next chair. Since Jim Hicks was the vice chair, he took charge of the meeting. We could have just appointed him as the chair, but instead, we decided to open up the floor for nominations. Jim and I were nominated for the position. We both had an opportunity to explain how we would conduct the board go-ing forward. My focus was on the healing process and starting anew. I do not recall what Jim said, but, usually, he was a man of few words. After a brief silence, some of the board members strongly urged us to learn from what happened over the past week and not to make this a deaf–hearing issue or take things personally. The discussion was civil and, in some ways, thought provoking; it also touched some raw nerves, which was under-standable after such a week.

After that, Jim and I were asked to leave the room, so I do not know what transpired during the deliberations among the board members. When they were ready for us, we came back into the room for the vote. The first vote resulted in a tie, eight votes for Jim and eight for me. I could sense, though, that some of the board members were understandably angry, and they may have voted for Jim (a hearing person) to send a message to the community. We took another vote, and this time, I was appointed chair effective immediately. My term would continue until the annual meeting in October, in accordance with the bylaws.

The weight of the world suddenly fell on my shoulders. I told the board that I accepted "this responsibility with deep humility." It was not a moment to celebrate but a moment to recollect, refresh, and restart while the rest of the world watched how Gallaudet moved forward. I then took the floor as chair and conducted the rest of the meeting. We still had a few remaining items that needed to be addressed, one of which was the protesters' demand that the board have a 51 percent deaf majority. At first glance, this seemed like a simple matter, but after further discussion, we realized that there were some legal issues that we needed to explore, including the language in the charter that established the university.

The board's bylaws at that time did not mention term limits, only that trustees should serve three-year terms that could run consecutively. This meant that we had to develop a procedure for reaching a 51 percent deaf majority, which involved asking the hearing trustees to resign to pave the way. We also had to make sure that there was nothing in the original Gallaudet charter and in the various congressional acts for Gallaudet over the years that would impede us from making this possible. Finally, we had to define *deaf*. The board decided to "authorize the chair to appoint a task force to study the composition and selection procedure for the board of trustees with a sensitivity toward enhancing representation on the board of those who are hearing impaired." The statement was carefully worded so as not to make us impotent if we agreed to the 51 percent majority and then encountered unforeseen obstacles during the review process.

Some of the board members were angry, and resignation was in the back of their minds. Alexander Patterson, Frank Sullivan, and Robert Sanderson implored them not to consider it at this time but to give it some thought. Any drastic changes would not help with the healing process that obviously needed to take place, and this request was heeded. One of the board members then made a motion to establish the task force, and it was approved.

At 5:00 p.m., the meeting was adjourned, but before we all went home, I thanked my fellow board members for what they had accomplished. It had been a very difficult and painful day of dealing with issues that no board would ever anticipate. To address them all in one day was a remarkable achievement. I believed that we had responded in a meaningful way to the events at hand.

The moment I came out of the meeting room, the world sort of fell on me. People were waiting to talk to me, but I needed some time to sort and organize my thoughts, so I headed for the men's room. I have always found this to be a good place to think—I go into a stall where no one can look at or try to talk to me. This gave me precious time to think things through, reflect on what had transpired that day, and prioritize the tasks that still had to be done. The first item on my list was to call I. King Jordan to offer him the presidency. The board was so confident he would accept the job that we didn't have a backup plan. In fact, most of the trustees had already left the hotel, so I don't know what I would have done if he had said no. Once I had his answer, I would contact the four student leaders because they needed to learn the news before the hearing public did. This was a symbolic but essential gesture. After all, the week had been about deaf people gaining control of their institution. People who have been oppressed for years can relate to this fact—the majority takes care of the majority before it takes care of the minority, which leaves the minority to take care of the minority.

When I came out of the men's room, I sat down with Myra Peabody of Peabody Fitzpatrick Communications. Up until now, I wasn't sure that Myra was the right person for the job because of what had happened the past week, especially on Wednesday when I was in her office. After a few minutes with her, though, she put me at ease, and we began to develop a plan for the evening. This plan had to be perfect, with things done in a specific order. If we missed one beat, the world would see it. I had to be sure we had a working TTY, and Lil was ready with not one but two.

Myra wanted me to talk to the press, but she wasn't aware that I hadn't contacted King yet. She said she would hold the press at bay and assist with drafting announcements both for me and for King to make to the world. My statement had to address how the board would respond to the protesters' demands. The first two were taken care of, and the board had agreed there would be no reprisals, but the 51 percent deaf majority still had to be resolved. I would have to explain that the board was committed to ensuring a deaf majority, but it would take some time to achieve. I had no clue as to whether the students and community would go along with that unfinished business.

I called King on the TTY, and his wife Linda answered. She said he was at the airport picking up a friend, and he would be back in an hour or so. This gave me the time I needed to grab a bite. I went to the hotel dining room with Robert and Frank, the only other board members who chose to hang around with me to witness the historic moment that was to evolve. We could see a lot of peeping toms looking through the windows of the hotel, so we were careful not to reveal any information about the board's decision. We didn't want anyone eavesdropping on our signs. The three of us were great supporters of each other—we worked together very well and we were very mindful of being in the minority on the board. Robert and Frank were 20 years my senior, and I learned a lot from those wise men. People asked us after DPN why we didn't play the "deaf" card. Our responses have been consistent—the institution of Gallaudet was the main concern, and we wanted the best, most qualified person to head Gallaudet. We preferred that this be a deaf person, but not because that person was deaf. We believed that if we played the "deaf" card, this would weaken the definition of deafness as a qualification.

King called me around 8:00, and I gave him the good news. He responded by saying, "I am delighted to hear the good news and thank you for sharing this." I asked him to come down to the hotel for the announcement, and he said, "sure." He asked me whether that he would have the board's support, and I assured him he would. We agreed that he would be at the hotel around 10 p.m. He told me later that he literally jumped up and down when he learned the news.

After hanging up with King, Myra asked whether I would talk to the press. I said "no" because I needed to speak with Greg Hlibok, the student leader first. Myra asked if I could do it after the announcement to the press, but my response was a firm no! Greg and the student leaders needed to hear the news first from me, not the press. I didn't want a repeat of the situation the previous Sunday when the campus learned about Zinser's selection from a press release. The student leaders were the heart of the protest, and they deserved to get the news firsthand.

Myra understood, so we went over the announcement and the plans for the rest of the evening. Then, I called Greg Hlibok at the Ole Jim, the alumni house that been the headquarters of the protest. Whoever answered the phone said Greg wasn't around and asked if he/she could take a message. I replied, "No, it has to be Greg." There was silence as people went scrambling all over campus to find him. When he finally came on, it immediately occurred to me that I had no way of verifying if it was really him. Hearing people can easily identify people by voice, but there was no way to see someone on a TTY.[17] I had to ask him some specific questions that only he could answer. Fortunately, Greg's family and my family had known each other for years, so this wouldn't be hard. Our conversation went like this:[18]

17. TTY was the vernacular used during that time. In the 1980s, TTY morphed into TDD. In the deaf community, we rarely used "TDD"; however, we used "TTY" all the time. TTY was short for "teletypewriter." TDD was short for "telecommunications device for the deaf."

18. This is how I remember the beginning of the conversation, and I confirmed it with Greg. The portion of the conversation where I indicated the choice of I. King Jordan as president is from *The Week the World*

Bravin: IS THIS GREG? GA

Hlibok: YES GA

Bravin: I NEED TO BE SURE IT'S YOU GREG. CAN YOU TELL ME THE NAMES OF MY 3 CHILDREN GA

Hlibok: JEFF, DEBBIE AND SETH GA

Bravin: GREAT, I'LL INDICATE THE NAMES OF YOUR SIBLINGS—BRUCE, STEVE AND NANCY GA

Hlibok: YES THAT IS CORRECT GA

Bravin: NOW THAT WE ARE SURE WHO WE ARE SPEAKING WITH, I SHALL PROCEED WITH WHAT I WANT TO TELL YOU GA

Hlibok: OK GA

Bravin: I WISH TO ANNOUNCE THE SELECTION OF

(typing)   I. KING JORDAN OF GALLAUDET AS THE NEW PRESIDENT JANE BASSETT SPILMAN RESIGNED (bedlam broke loose among the Ole Jim crowd, causing static) TASK FORCE ON COMPOSITION OF DEAF PEOPLE AND NO REPRISALS GA

Hlibok   WONDERFUL WANT TO BE SURE JORDAN IS

(typing)   PERMANENT OR INTERIM QQ GA

Bravin: PERMANENT GA

On learning this news, the crowd in Ole Jim let out another roar, causing more static on the TDD. "Quiet! Quiet" commanded Hlibok.

Hlibok: WHO IS CHAIR OF BOARD NOW Q GA

Bravin: I AM GA

Heard Gallaudet by Jack R. Gannon (Gallaudet University Press, 1989), 142–43.

More shouting. "Quiet, Quiet," people in the crowd reminded each other.

Hlibok: SPILMAN RESIGNED AS CHAIR OR AS MEMBER Q GA

Bravin: BOTH GA

Another uproar from the onlookers. More static on the TDD.

Hlibok: TIME FRAME FOR TASK FORCE Q GA

Bravin: WORKING ON IT AND WILL APPOINT MEMBERS TOMORROW WILL ANNOUNCE IT TOMORROW GA

Hlibok: IF YOU HAVE TIME ARE YOU WILLING TO MEET ME ASAP Q GA

Bravin: WILL MAKE PRESS ANNOUNCEMENT AFTER THIS GA (It was 7:52 p.m.)

Hlibok: THANKS APPRECIATE IT LAST QUESTION WHAT WILL BE MAKE UP OF TASK FORCE QQ GA

Bravin: (Static appeared on Bravin's end.) REPEAT ALL NUMBERS GA

Hlibok repeated his question.

Bravin: YET TO BE DETERMINED BUT MAJORITY WILL BE DEAF GA

Hlibok: GREAT ANYTIME YOU WANT TO SPEAK TO ME SEND SECURITY WE ARE ELATED GA

Bravin: CORRECT Q EVERYTHING WILL BE BACK TO NORMAL [on campus] Q GA

Hlibok: YES WE WILL GET EVERYTHING BACK TO NORMAL BUT NEED TO TALK ABOUT THIS AND COUNCIL WILL MEET AFTERWARD GA

Bravin: ASKING FOR A PRESS RELEASE ASSUMING ARE THINGS BACK TO NORMAL Q GA

Hlibok: YES WE HAVE NO DOUBT THINGS WILL
           BE BACK TO NORMAL BUT NEED TO TALK
           FIRST GA

Bravin: CANNOT BE IN A POSITION TO WAIT FOR
           YOU GA

Hlibok put Bravin on hold while he conferred with Jeff
Rosen, who was a lawyer, and Jerry Covell, one of the four
student leaders, and then answered: UNIVERSITY WILL BE
OPEN ON OUR FAITH THAT YOU WILL TALK WITH US
ABOUT THE TASK FORCE COMPRISED OF MAJORITY
OF DEAF PEOPLE GA

Bravin: DEAF TRUSTEES RIGHT Q GA
Hlibok: RIGHT GA
Bravin: CAN ASSURE YOU OF THIS GA
Hlibok: HOLD THANK YOU SO HAVE A GOOD EVE-
           NING GA TO SK SK
Bravin: GREG MEET ME AT THE PRESIDENTS OFFICE
           AT 9 AM TOMORROW AND UNLOCK EVERY-
           THING GA
Hlibok: FINE GA OR SK
Bravin: SK SK SK

After the call to Greg, it was time to share the news with
the world. Myra and I went over the announcement several
times again before we went upstairs to the main lobby of the
hotel, where I would deliver my statement. In order for us to
get to the podium that had been set up, we had to walk up the
service stairs into the hotel kitchen and then into the lobby.
Needless to say, I was nervous—this was one of the biggest
public moments of my life. When I opened the door into the
lobby, I saw the podium, replete with microphones. The lobby
was filled with reporters, students, and members of the Gallaudet and deaf communities. To my surprise, Jane also was there,

looking like she was waiting for me. I had not seen her since she left the board meeting earlier that day. The television lights went up as soon as Jane and I walked to the podium.

Myra started the session off by stating that the board of trustees had a statement to make. I was standing next to Jane watching Myra and the interpreter. Then, Myra introduced me, and I walked to the podium. I realized I was in front of the microphones, which I would not be able to use very well, so I switched places with the interpreter. I started by saying, "My name is Philip W. Bravin. I represent the Gallaudet Board of Trustees as its new chair. I have several announcements to make. Today, we have regretfully accepted the resignation of Jane Bassett Spilman as chairman of the Gallaudet University Board of Trustees. She has a statement to make."

Myra Peabody introducing Phil Bravin and Jane Spilman at the Embassy Row hotel prior to the announcement of the results of the board meeting. Jan Nishimura is the interpreter on the right. Courtesy of the Gallaudet University Video Library.

The author making several announcements to the public about the results of the board meeting on Sunday. Note that the microphones were not used by Phil, but rather by the interpreter, Sheila Deane. Courtesy of the Gallaudet University Video Library.

The author flashes the I LOVE YOU sign to Jane Spilman after she made her announcement that she was stepping down as chair and from the board. Sheila Deane is the interpreter on the left. Courtesy of the Gallaudet Video Library.

Jane walked to the podium and told the crowd that she had resigned as chair of the board and resigned from the board. She went on to say that "in the eyes of some people, I have become an obstacle to the future of the university," and she felt it was in the best interests of Gallaudet to remove that obstacle. She also acknowledged the courage of the student leaders, referring to them by their first names, Greg (Hlibok), Tim (Rarus), Bridgetta (Bourne), and Jerry (Covell).

After Jane completed her remarks, I returned to the podium and said "Thank you, Jane" for all she had done for Gallaudet, and I flashed her the I LOVE YOU sign. Then, it was time to make the long-awaited announcement, that the Gallaudet University Board of Trustees had selected I. King Jordan as the eighth president of the university. I went on to say that I had already spoken with Dr. Jordan and shared the good news with him, and I announced that the board would form a task force to create a plan for restructuring the board so that a majority of trustees would be deaf. I explained that the board would not impose any sanctions on the students, faculty, and staff for participating, or not participating, in the protest. And, I said that I told Greg about Jordan's election, and he, as president of the SBG, promised that "the campus will be back to normal, not by tomorrow, but now."

Looking out at the audience before me, I saw many people crying and clapping and waving their hands, including members of the media. Seeing some reporters in tears and others clapping made me realize they had been in tune with the students and the deaf community that week. I concluded my remarks by saying, "Thank you. Gallaudet will sail on to greater waters."

The press conference ended, and Myra, Jane, and I went our separate ways. In fact, that was the last time I saw Jane.[19] She never did congratulate me on my selection as chair.

---

19. There were two instances of contact since 1988. When I was very ill after surgery for stomach cancer in 1992, I received a big bouquet of

After an hour or so, I welcomed King into my room at the hotel, so we could go over the public announcement we were going to make. I felt it was important for us to develop good chemistry—we needed to have a meeting of the minds and align our individual visions. We achieved this and more; that night was the beginning of a wonderful and collegial relationship.

Soon it was time for us to go downstairs to deliver our joint statement. King's wife Linda and his children, King and Heidi, came with us. We found out that the crowd waiting for us was

I. King Jordan making a statement to the public after being introduced by me. Jordan is signing ACCEPT, which was the first part of his statement, "I am thrilled to accept the invitation of the board of trustees to become the president of Gallaudet University." His wife Linda is on the right. The person behind King is Richard Keil, a reporter for the Associated Press who was an omnipresent figure on campus during DPN. Courtesy of the Gallaudet University Archives.

flowers in my hospital room. The card read, "Get well soon, Jane Spilman." I kept sending her annual holiday messages from my family since then and still do to this day. About five years ago, I received a handwritten card from her, thanking me for all the messages and letting me know she had moved to Richmond and was doing well. I have never met or seen her in person since 1988.

too large for the hotel to handle in the lobby, so the staff set up a makeshift podium outside. When King, Linda, and I walked outside, the crowd chanted in sign language "King, King, King." We went to the podium, and I introduced King as the new president of Gallaudet. He then said,

> I am thrilled to accept the invitation of the Board of Trustees to become the president of Gallaudet University. It is a historic moment for deaf people around the world. In this week we can truly say that we, together and united, have overcome our own reluctance to stand for our rights and our full representation. The world has watched the deaf community come of age. We will no longer accept limits on what we can achieve.
>
> It is a gratifying moment for me personally. I have worked and cared deeply for Gallaudet University since I came to teach psychology in 1973. My desire to contribute more has increased with each opportunity I've had to contribute.
>
> As the new president of a newly energized university, given the determination and courage of students and faculty in recent days, given the responsible actions of individuals and the Board since the world first heard the roar from the Gallaudet campus, given the great cooperative spirit that makes us a community— hearing and deaf—I am confident we can walk boldly into a future without artificial limits.
>
> And I must give the highest praise to the students of Gallaudet for showing us all exactly how even now one can seize an idea with such force of argument that it becomes a reality.
>
> Thank you.[20]

Pandemonium followed! King went to the campus with his family to be with his new "followers." I quietly retreated to my hotel room, took off my tie, and said to myself, "What a day;

---

20. I. King Jordan, "Statement of Dr. I. King Jordan, President, Gallaudet University," March 13, 1988. Courtesy of the author's personal files.

Phil Bravin's sister, Sherry, and their dad, Carl, Courtesy of the Gallaudet University Video Library.

what a week!" I wanted my wife to get all the news directly from me, so I went to the TTY and called her, but she already knew that I had become chair of the board. My sister, Sherry, who was on the staff at Gallaudet, had told her. Judy congratulated me and told me it felt funny seeing me on television and learning again of my selection rather than hearing it from me. I had to explain that the circumstances just did not make this possible. Unbeknownst to me, I found out the next day that my dad, sister Sherry, and my son Jeff were celebrating with the campus community at Ole Jim[21] that night with Greg Hlibok and King. This closed the loop that had not been closed between my family and me during the movement.

---

21. Ole Jim was the name of the campus building that was the "Old Gym" built in the late 1800s. It was the first facility with an indoor (unheated) swimming pool in the Washington, DC, area. It currently houses the alumni office of Gallaudet.

"The Silent World's Rebellion for Civil Rights." Front page of the
Washington Post on March 13, 1988. From The Washington Post.
© 1988 The Washington Post. All rights reserved. Used under license.
http://www.washingtonpost.com.

9

Monday, March 14

When I woke up Monday morning, the first thing I did was pick up the *Washington Post* outside my hotel room door. The front page said it all, "Gallaudet U. Selects First Deaf President," with the subhead "Board Chief Resigns, Student Demands Met."[22] In the article, Greg Hlibok was quoted as saying, "We got five demands, not just four." My selection as chair was the bonus since a deaf chair was not part of the four original demands. Going down for breakfast, I scooped up a copy of *USA Today* and saw my picture in the paper.[23] Never in a thousand years would I imagine seeing myself in a newspaper. It dawned on me that the world would have its eyes on Gallaudet.

After breakfast, I took a cab from the Embassy Row Hotel to the campus. Looking around, I was amazed at how pristine it was—as if nothing had happened during that past week. Spring was in the air in Washington, and some of the greenery was starting to bloom. I walked over to the EMG building, where the president's office was located on the second floor. King was in his office, so I went in and gave him a hug. We sat down on the sofa to chat while we waited for Greg Hlibok. The room was bare, with nothing on the walls, and no papers or magazines were lying around. But the setting was very symbolic.

---

22. Molly Sinclair, "Gallaudet U. Selects First Deaf President," *Washington Post*, March 14, 1988.

23. Peter Johnson, "Deaf College Vibrates with Victory," *USA Today*, March 14, 1988.

When Greg arrived, he commented that "for the first time in Gallaudet's history, the students, the president, and the chairman of the board were able to meet without using an interpreter." This was a very powerful and true statement; it sent chills up my spine. (I did some research and found that no chair of the board before me was able to communicate in sign language.) I thanked Greg for putting the campus back in order, and then we went over the events of the previous week. Since I had been excluded from the campus most of the week, I needed to understand the dynamics that prevailed to better perform my role going forward.

After Greg left, King and I looked each other in the eyes and asked ourselves "What next?" After all, we were in uncharted territory. In normal circumstances, when a new president is selected, the board chair would already have been around for some time. Conversely, when a new board chair starts his or her term, the president would already have been in the job. The first question that came to our minds was what our legal roles were. We knew that the board bylaws defined these, but there were areas that the bylaws did not address, such as what the board chair can and can't do and what the president can and can't do. We sent out a request for one of Gallaudet's attorneys to come to campus and explain things to us. King and I agreed that we had to start reassuring the world that everything was under control. The way to do it was to be in touch with Gallaudet's stakeholders by giving talks and meeting with them face to face. We realized that we, but especially King, were in a fishbowl. The protest had put us on the map (and a pedestal), and King was now the face of Gallaudet. Many people were waiting to see how we would handle our new roles.

We then went over to Ole Jim to meet with the faculty, staff, community members, and alumni leaders of the protest. When we walked in, the group of about twenty gave us a standing ovation. This hit me hard—up to that point, I was just a person who came on campus with a well-intentioned role, to support Gallaudet. The idea of being a public figure was the last thing I expected, and I knew King felt the same. The group asked us questions, including when the board would have a 51 percent deaf majority. I reiterated that Greg and I had agreed that this would take some time, but that the task force would soon begin working on it.

Later, Myra Peabody strongly recommended that we have a press conference to provide closure for the week and allow us to move on with our normal business. She told us the press was on standby and wanted to be able to ask questions of King, Greg, and me. We agreed to do it later that afternoon in Ely Auditorium. To prepare, Greg, King, and I met to discuss the plan for the press conference—we decided to appear jointly as a group and to determine at the time whether to answer questions together or individually.

After King and I left Ole Jim, the Gallaudet attorney, Scott Kragie, came over to review the bylaws with us and clarify our roles. He emphasized that the bottom line was that the board was responsible for the university and for hiring the president, who took take care of the university's day-to-day operations for the board. Scott outlined the normal responsibilities of the chair and president and shared with us the congressional and federal oversight roles and how they compared with the board's role.

When it was time for the press conference, King, Greg, and I met at Ely Auditorium. Greg sat between King and me to show support for the students. The view from the stage was a sight to behold. Many national news and broadcast TV correspondents were in the audience, and there were twenty or so TV cameras set up in the back of the auditorium. Photographers roamed through the aisles. It reminded me of a presidential news conference.

Bravin, Jordan, and Hlibok on stage at a press conference on Monday, March 14. Courtesy of the Gallaudet University Archives.

A Gallaudet staff member moderated the press conference. She selected people from the audience to ask questions. Some of the questions were directed to all three of us, and some to each of us individually. During that conference, King made the statement that was to follow him for years to come: "Deaf people can do anything that hearing people can, except hear."

I couldn't answer some of the questions directed at me because they asked for confidential information that I didn't think should be revealed. However, the question of the 51 percent deaf majority on the board came up again. I explained that the task force would be composed of a majority of deaf trustees and that it would work out the procedures and timetable for achieving this. The press conference lasted close to an hour, and, as Myra had predicted, it brought closure to the past week's events.

After the press conference, I went back to the president's office to collect my things. Before I could leave, we received requests for interviews from the TV stations in Washington. All three of the local network affiliate stations (ABC, CBS, and NBC) wanted to interview King and me separately on the evening news. I couldn't be in three places at once, so the stations agreed to interview me via a remote hookup. We set up a schedule that went something like this: 5:04 with one station, 5:10 with the second, and 5:17 with the third, but this plan was complicated by the logistics. The three trucks were parked side by side in the front of the campus, with Chapel Hall and the Tower Clock as a backdrop. The problem was this: Since I didn't use my voice to speak, my interpreter, Jan, would voice for me, but the camera would be on me, not her. Also, we didn't have a video feed to the studio, so I wouldn't be able to see the news anchor. This meant Jan had to wear a headset to hear the news anchor and use a microphone to voice for me.

To prepare for the interviews, several things had to happen—the camera had to be checked to be sure the lighting was good and I was visible; Jan had to be sure she could hear the news anchor; and the news anchor had to be able to hear Jan speaking. A test link had to be in place prior to each interview. When the test was validated, the technical crew had to communicate to the studio that the interview was ready to begin. During the transition from one story to another at the studio, my interview would be "cut in" and become live.

What we didn't realize was that the time between interviews was pretty tight, and we didn't take into account the test link phase. But we went along anyway. During my interview with the first station, the crew from the second station stood next to the crew doing the first interview. As soon as the interview was done, someone ripped off the mike and headset from poor Jan while the second crew came on and put another mike and headset on her and then tested the link. If the test didn't work as expected, they had to make adjustments before we went on air.

Being interviewed by TV stations. The interviews took place in front of the campus (near the Gallaudet statue) after the press conference. The interpreter was Jan Nishimura who had to deal with the microphones and headsets. Courtesy of the Gallaudet University Archives.

I remained calm during the interviews without revealing the chaos taking place off camera. The third interview was delayed somewhat, so Jan and I waited in the truck and chatted with the crew. I took it upon myself to ask the crew what they thought of the week. After some small talk, they explained to me that they were the "protest unit" for that station, and their job was to go all over town to report on the various protests that are a mainstay of a capital city like Washington. What was different and unique to the crew was that the protesters had won. This struck me as something quite profound—it's not often that a protest produces successful results. In retrospect, it was not just that the protesters had won, but a paradigm shift had occurred.

As soon as the interviews ended, I collected my things and got a ride to National Airport for the flight back home to my wife and children. Unlike the week before, I didn't feel defeated, but I didn't feel victorious either. Rather, I had a sense of satisfaction at how things evolved. They could have been much worse, but the pendulum swung from anger and frustration to the elation and optimism that carried Gallaudet a long way in the days, months, and years that followed. Deaf people had begun the process of taking control of their destiny out of the hands of hearing people.

"Gallaudet U. Selects First Deaf President." Front page of the
Washington Post on March 14, 1988. From The Washington Post.
© 1988 The Washington Post. All rights reserved. Used under license.
http://www.washingtonpost.com.

Epilogue

The impact of the DPN movement cannot be underestimated. In the weeks, months, and years following DPN, the United States and countries around the world began to acknowledge and ensure the rights of deaf and disabled people through policy changes at the local, national, and international levels. In this epilogue, I outline just a few such events and changes at Gallaudet and in the United States.

COMMUNICATING WITH I. KING JORDAN

When two hearing people converse over the phone, they usually are able to identify the other party by recognizing their respective voices. Before the advent of video communication, deaf people typed back and forth using a teletypewriter (TTY). With such a device, as I mentioned earlier, there is no real way for deaf people to verify the identity of the other party other than using passwords.

When King and I were elected to our positions, we realized very quickly that we needed to communicate frequently over the phone via TTY. We, of course, were mindful of our highly visible positions and that anything we said would come under a magnifying glass. For that reason, we had to identify ourselves with passwords at the beginning of our conversations.

When we discussed which passwords we would be using, we decided on something that was personal and described our way of life. King, being an avid marathon and 100-mile runner, chose the term *Fleet*. I loved Vermont so much I wanted something that related to Vermont but would not pinpoint where we had our second home. So I chose *Stowe*, a well-known ski resort about 100 miles north of our place in Chester.

The conversations usually began something like this: When I called King, he would answer, "King here, GA." I would then respond with, "This is Stowe, how are you these days? GA." King would then type, "Fleet here, great to hear from you." The passwords gave us the peace of mind we needed to talk freely. Those conversations usually took place weekly during the evening for an hour or so, and then became biweekly over time. We have protected the identity of those passwords for all these years, and we have agreed to make them public with the publication of this book. Primitive as this system was, it served our purpose.

GALLAUDET'S RELATIONSHIP WITH CONGRESS

In the weeks after the DPN movement, the campus was quiet and returned back to normal operations. One of King's first responsibilities was to appear in front of Congress at a hearing on the report of the Commission on Education of the Deaf.[1] This commission, chaired by Dr. Frank Bowe, had taken a hard and comprehensive look at deaf education in America.

Several weeks later, King was in front of Congress again, testifying before both the Senate and House appropriations committees that had oversight on funding for Gallaudet, Howard University, the National Technical Institute for the Deaf (Rochester Institute of Technology [RIT]), and the American Printing House for the Blind. Up until this time, King had had limited, if any, encounters with Congress. I attended those sessions with him to show Congress that matters were under control and to reassure the committee members that Gallaudet was "on a roll." This was a "baptism by fire" for King. Those sessions required a lot of preparation and getting acquainted with those people.

One of the more interesting exchanges a year or so later occurred when Congressman Joseph Early of Massachusetts asked whether Gallaudet's budget included covering the cost

---

1. *Hearing on H.R. Rep. 100, Before the Subcomm. on the Select Education of the Comm. on Education and Labor,* 100th Cong., 2nd session.

of interpreting services for King and me. While this was unexpected, it gave me an inkling that the congressman saw the sea change of how the rest of the world looked at us in a different light. It was easy to see how awed and respectful Congress was to King after the events of DPN. There was nary a negative comment from anyone, and that remained true for Gallaudet's relationship with Congress for most of King's tenure. The hearings were pro forma sessions—most of the questions were discussed in advance—but this was how things worked. Very rarely did we get an unexpected question that we could not answer, but when we did, we sent the responses later, and they were entered into the record. Congressmen Bonior and Gunderson, who were still on the board of trustees, were faithful to Gallaudet, and they prefaced our appearances at such hearings with introductory comments.

Senator John McCain was another friend of the deaf and disabled community. I first heard him speak at the National Association of the Deaf (NAD) conference in Charleston, SC, in July 1988, where he was the keynote speaker. In his speech, he assured the attendees of the conference that he would stand and fight for the communication rights of deaf people because of his experience as a prisoner of war in Vietnam. He told us that the guards did not allow the American soldiers to talk to each other, lest they be tortured for doing so. McCain and his fellow prisoners then devised a code by knocking on the walls and pipes in a code, so they could communicate with one another. He said this was one of the reasons he kept his sanity for the seven years in captivity.[2]

His presence at the NAD conference was the beginning of a long relationship with Gallaudet that started when Timothy Rarus, one of the DPN student leaders, worked as an intern

---

2. While there is no recorded transcript of his remarks at the NAD conference, the author is reciting this from the best of his recollection, as he was in the room where it took place.

in his office. Subsequently, McCain became one of the main and original cosponsors of the Americans with Disabilities Act, and he spoke eloquently on matters related to accessibility and communication in his years on Capitol Hill. He joined the Gallaudet University Board of Trustees in 1995 as a public member representing the Senate and served for eleven years. I had the privilege of meeting him several times during my tenure on the board.

ACHIEVING A 51 PERCENT DEAF MAJORITY ON THE BOARD OF TRUSTEES

The demand from the protesters that the board be at least 51 percent deaf was more of a challenge than everyone had believed. While the goal was necessary, the process dictated otherwise.

I had announced at my first press conference as chair that I would appoint a task force to study the composition of and the procedures for selecting members of the board of trustees. I had also promised Greg Hlibok that the task force would have a deaf majority. This meant that the three other deaf trustees—Robert Sanderson, Frank Sullivan, and Harvey Corson—were automatically part of the committee. I went over the list of the remaining hearing members and chose Alexander Patterson (because he knew the bylaws inside and out) and Judge Thomas Penfield Jackson (because of his legal background and his steadfast fairness and impartiality). I didn't think I should chair this committee, so I appointed Robert Sanderson chair of the task force due to his wide background in the community and his experience as president of the National Association of the Deaf.

The Gallaudet Public Relations office sent out a press release on May 9, 1988, with my statement about the task force.[3]

3. Gallaudet University, "Task Force Named to Study Gallaudet University Board," press release, May 9, 1988.

It was crafted carefully to avoid any reading between the lines. In it, I explained that "the task force was created in response to a growing concern that there was not adequate representation from the deaf community on the board. With the board's authorization, I have appointed a task force that will take a serious look at the board's composition and selection procedures with the goal of eventually composing the board with a majority of deaf members." Privately, I told Robert to move with deliberate speed—not to take any shortcuts, but to be as thorough and legal as possible.

In the meantime, one of my challenges after the protest was to handle a demoralized board of trustees. During the Sunday meeting at the Embassy Row Hotel, where we selected King as the eighth president, I could sense that some of the board members felt angry and did not quite want to give in at the outset; but after further discussion, reality set in. However, for certain members, the hidden feelings carried over into the next few months. I felt it was time for us to have closure on the whole thing and to regroup and move forward. The timing was critical. I didn't want to do it during the school year, nor too close to commencement, to take away from the levity that usually surrounds that time of the year. I also wanted to do it before King was formally installed as president. I discussed this matter with Myra Peabody, who we retained as our public relations consultant after the events of the protest week. I, for one, appreciated how Myra handled the end of the protest week after I was installed as chair, and she was quick to pick up the nuances of the deaf community.

I aired the thought of a retreat to Myra and King, and we discussed and agreed that there was a need to take the air out of the bag and start anew. Some board members considered resigning, but I talked them out of it, making the point that we hadn't had a postmortem discussion or regrouped after the protest. I'm a student of "counting to 100," not reacting immediately, but thinking things through and letting the dust settle before dealing with whatever matter was at hand. Myra came up with the concept of calling our meeting an *advance* rather than a *retreat* because *retreat* would send the wrong signal, as if we were retreating from the events of the protest week. *Advance* put a positive spin on our discussions, and she believed it would lead us to look forward rather than look back.

We met on a weekend in late August 1988 at a resort in Northern Virginia with Myra as the facilitator. Basically, we laid down the items that were obstacles—the feeling of being out of touch with the community and whether the protest would cast a negative light on Gallaudet—and discussed how to remove those obstacles and free the way for us to move forward. Some board members came to me during the weekend to express their thoughts, and some offered to step down to make way for more deaf trustees. This was a commendable act on their part.

As a result of the advance, we gave each board member a TTY, instituted basic deaf culture sessions during each board meeting, and offered optional ASL classes for those who would be interested. The hidden feelings and agendas began to disappear, the board functioned with far better dynamics, and our discussions became much more substantive and productive.

The task force on the 51 percent deaf majority, which had begun to meet in the spring, continued to meet during the summer, but we primarily communicated via mail. At the October 1988 board meeting, we gave a status report and handed out our suggested changes to the bylaws and a "Resolution for Year 125."[4] We thought this would give the board time to digest the material and be prepared to vote on the bylaw changes at the February 1989 meeting. During the October meeting, Eloise Thornberry, the wife of former US Senator Homer Thornberry of Texas, became the first board member to announce that she

---

4. Gallaudet University Board of Trustees, "Resolution for Year 125," October 1988, unpublished document. Courtesy of the author's personal files.

was ready to give up her seat for a deaf board member. Senator Thornberry, who was a close friend of Lyndon B. Johnson, had been a board member during Dr. Elstad's tenure, and he paved the way for Congress to appropriate funds for Gallaudet's major expansion in the 1950s and 1960s. Eloise passed away in April 1989. I flew to Austin to attend her funeral and gravesite service. I was the only Gallaudet representative invited to the gravesite service at the Texas State Cemetery.

At the February 1989 meeting, the board discussed the bylaws and the resolution. Some hearing board members thought that the resolution was sufficient without the bylaw changes. The deaf members felt we needed the "force of law" with the bylaws, rather than trust in a good-faith process if we adopted the resolution. When we voted on changes, there were four affirmative votes, three no votes, and four abstentions. Since this did not constitute the two-thirds vote needed to amend the bylaws, the changes were not adopted. The board then made some minor changes, and the bylaws addressing the 51 percent deaf composition were adopted at the May 1989 meeting.

There were some difficult issues we had to deal with pertaining to the bylaws. The first was that we had to be sure that none of the changes were in conflict with the enabling legislation passed by Congress. The second was the definition of *deaf or hard of hearing*, which we decided to leave as a generic term. The third was how to word the mandate on the 51 percent deaf majority. During our deliberations, the Gallaudet attorney described a hypothetical situation in which we had a majority of eleven deaf and hard of hearing board members and two either passed away or resigned between meetings. He explained that this would make the board legally impotent if the bylaws specifically stated the "majority shall be deaf or hard of hearing." We realized we had to word the bylaws carefully, and we came up with the following provision: "A majority of the Voting Trustees shall be deaf or hard of hearing; provided, however, that failure to maintain a majority who are deaf or hard of hearing shall not diminish the Board's authority to act on any matter which may come before it." Once all the concerns were addressed, the final DPN demand was finally resolved.

After the May 1989 meeting, we added two deaf members to the Board—Dr. Glenn Anderson, a professor at the University of Arkansas at Little Rock, and Dr. Carol Padden, a professor at the University of California, San Diego. In October 1989, Frank Sullivan, one of the long-standing deaf members, stepped down. As a result, we added John Yeh, a deaf business executive, and Ken Levinson, a certified public accountant and then president of the Alexander Graham Bell Association of the Deaf. In the following year, some of the hearing board members resigned or did not renew their terms to make way for the deaf members. This was a commendable gesture on their part. By 1991, we finally reached a 51 percent majority of deaf board members. Looking back, achieving all this in the span of three years was something we should be proud of.

Subsequent to our changes, some deaf education programs and nonprofit organizations in the United States took it upon themselves to mandate deaf majorities on their respective boards.

RESOLUTION FOR YEAR 125[5]

WHEREAS, the primary mission of Gallaudet University is, and shall continue to be, the education of the deaf for a lifetime of optimum participation in the affairs of society; and

WHEREAS, an integral part of such an education is the provision of maximum opportunity for the deaf to participate fully in matters of governance of the institution; and

WHEREAS, the momentous events of March 1988 have demonstrated to the Trustees the necessity of expanding the

---

5. Judge Jackson was the primary author of this resolution. We defined *deaf* to mean those persons who primarily use visual means of communication, such as sign language, fingerspelling, lipreading/speechreading, and writing.

opportunities for the deaf for such participation, and, the Board of Trustees being the governing body of Gallaudet University;

BE IT THEREFORE RESOLVED, that the Board of Trustees pledges itself to so constitute itself that the number of its deaf members shall be the maximum number possible consistent with its responsibilities for the proper governance of the institution; and it is

FURTHER RESOLVED, that the Trustees acknowledge that their terms of service on the Board are finite, and that election thereto imports no right to re-election upon the expiration, or the indefinite extension, of a term of service thereon; and it is

FURTHER RESOLVED, that, henceforth, upon the expiration of a term of service of a hearing Trustee, or the resignation from office of a hearing Trustee, the Board shall promptly fill the vacancy so created with a duly qualified successor who is deaf, unless the Board shall by majority vote expressly determine that it is to the greater benefit of the institution to elect the same or another hearing Trustee to the position than to elect a deaf candidate; and it is

FURTHER RESOLVED, that the foregoing preference shall be extended to deaf candidates for election to the Board until such time as the deaf members of the Board shall constitute a majority thereof; and it is

FURTHER RESOLVED, that there is re-established, as a standing committee of the Board, a Committee on Trustees, who shall be appointed annually by the Chair of the Board, whose duty shall be to identify qualified candidates for election to the Board of Trustees, and who shall execute such duty with due regard for the premises of the Resolution.

THE INAUGURATION OF I. KING JORDAN AS THE EIGHTH PRESIDENT OF GALLAUDET UNIVERSITY

I. King Jordan's formal installation as the first deaf president of Gallaudet took place on a rainy day in October 1988. The rain that day was heavy but did not take one iota away from the happiness and festiveness of the occasion. King worked very hard on his inauguration speech, knowing that everyone would analyze it with a magnifying glass. I also was a bit nervous, knowing that this was a momentous day. We were going to prove to the world that deaf people can fill leadership roles.

The Field House was filled with Gallaudet students, faculty, staff, and alumni, as well as representatives from many colleges and universities and members of the media. Greg Hlibok, who was still president of the SBG, sat among the dignitaries on the stage. There also was a satellite hookup to Gallaudet's regional centers, schools for the deaf all over the country, and some international centers. The inauguration program began with representatives of the Gallaudet community and the deaf community, including the popular president of the Gallaudet University Alumni Association, Gerald "Bummy" Burstein, and the president of the National Association of the Deaf, Larry Newman, giving opening remarks. When Bummy came to the podium to present his remarks, he noticed that he had two ASL interpreters, one on each side of the stage. Quick witted as he always was, he said, "I note I have two interpreters, the one on the left is my woofer, and the one on my right is the tweeter." That brought down the house.

After all the greetings, a group of students from the Kendall Demonstration Elementary School, the Model Secondary School for the Deaf, and the university performed a song. Then, one of the younger boys gave a gift to King, which brought him on the verge of tears.

Senator Tom Harkin (D-IA), who has a deaf brother, was the keynote speaker. He opened his remarks by saying, "When I was in Europe this summer, I was approached by a small group of deaf people who asked me about the president. They weren't interested in Ronald Reagan; they wanted to know about the new president of Gallaudet." That was substantial—attesting to the fact that deaf people everywhere looked to King and

Gallaudet after DPN; the lid of oppression was starting to leak. He concluded his speech with the assertion that "no more will deaf people tolerate the paternalism and charity of those who seek to control your future. You are the masters of your own destiny."[6]

When it was time to install King as president, I gave a few remarks and then formally pronounced, "With the authority vested in me by the board of trustees of Gallaudet University, I now install you as the eighth president—and the first deaf president—of Gallaudet University." I then presented the Presidential Medallion to King, putting it over his neck, placed my hands on his chest for a moment, and gave him a long, warm handshake. Everyone all over the Field House stood up, applauded, and cheered. The world was on King's shoulders, so to speak. I then went on to say that "King set foot on his Plymouth Rock when he set foot at Gallaudet as a student in 1968, and that path since then would lead to his appointment as president, but the path doesn't stop here. The new path he'll be building will be the path all deaf people will tread in the years to come."

Then it came time for King to present his inaugural speech, "Let Us Begin Together." He began the speech by acknowledging his wife Linda as his harshest critic, his trusted advisor, and his best friend. He thanked her for her help, good counsel, infinite patience, and understanding. Then he set the stage for the speech by stating, "Last March, we put our hands to the ground, and we felt the vibrations of generations of aspirations and expectations." In a reference to the football huddle, which was invented at Gallaudet in the late 1890s, he concluded his speech with these words, "We came out of our huddle, and we made a beginning. And now, let us begin together."[7]

---

6. Tom Harkin (IA), "Remarks of Senator Tom Harkin, Inauguration of President I. King Jordan," Cong. Rec. 134, pt. 23 (1988): 32597.

7. Tom Harkin (IA), "Inauguration of I. King Jordan to the Presidency of Gallaudet University," Cong. Rec. 134, pt. 23 (1988): 32596–97.

Bravin congratulates Jordan after giving him the Presidential
Medallion at his inauguration. Reprinted from *Gallaudet Today*
(Winter 1988/1989): 11.

It rained so hard, it felt like the skies were crying with joy.
I recall very well, a few years afterward, I asked some people
on campus if they remembered what the weather was like on
King's inauguration day. Most forgot the rain, saying it was
"sunny, such a beautiful day."

THE KELLOGG CONFERENCE CENTER

The Kellogg Foundation has a special history with Gallaudet. Its first contribution was a grant for Gallaudet's Special Schools of the Future project during Dr. Merrill's tenure, and the project leader was Dr. Roz Rosen. The concept started with the passage of Public Law 94-142, the Education for All Handicapped Children Act, which guaranteed a free appropriate public education to each child with a disability.[8] Dr. Merrill was mindful of the impact it would have on schools for the deaf in the United States. The grant funded the dissemination of information and training materials about how schools could implement the changes mandated by the law. This project was so successful that, in the mid-1980s, Kellogg and Gallaudet started discussions for a follow-up project.

After King assumed the presidency, Dr. Jim Hicks, a board member, told King he felt we would have a development opportunity with Kellogg since he knew the chair, Dr. Russell Mawby, very well due to their common interest in agriculture. Hicks encouraged King to go to the Kellogg headquarters in Battle Creek, MI, to meet Mawby. He said we could make the trip to Battle Creek for a two-hour meeting without an agenda just to get to know the folks at Kellogg, and then we could return the next time with an "ask."

King, Phil Sprinkle, Jim Hicks, and I flew out to Battle Creek in June 1989 for the meeting. King, true to his discipline and focus, did a hard run the morning of the meeting. The meeting started off very congenially, and I sensed Mawby and his staff were extremely interested in the Gallaudet story and King himself. The two-hour time limit was scrapped, and we continued through lunch. Mawby brought more of his staff into the conference room.

---

8. To amend the Education for All Handicapped Children Act to provide educational assistance to all handicapped children, and for other purposes, P.L. 94-142, 89 Stat. 773 (1975).

King was totally prepared for the meeting and was able to answer questions and articulate his vision for Gallaudet, but he was mindful of avoiding the "ask." Toward the end of the day, as it turned out, Russell Mawby asked King what Gallaudet needed for its programs. King was not quite prepared for this specific question; however, he responded that Gallaudet could use a conference center, so that the university and organizations in the DC area could host conferences on campus, which, in turn, would benefit the educational programs at Gallaudet. The Kellogg Conference Hotel on campus is a result of this visit, thanks to the $13 million gift from the Kellogg Foundation.

While the hotel was being designed, King and I discussed the idea of having the boardroom situated there. The then-existing room in the EMG building on campus was a nice room, but it was very narrow and not deaf friendly. It had a long rectangular table, and the deaf members usually sat on the same side, so we could see the interpreters. But this arrangement made it difficult for us to see each other signing. Having lived with that situation for so long, I made the decision that there would no longer be a "deaf row" at such meetings. Deaf and hearing attendees should feel free to sit wherever they wanted. The way to do it was to create a circular table so that everyone could see the interpreter and the other board members anywhere in the room.

Off we went to implement our idea. Roz Rosen, who was then the dean of the College for Continuing Education, was a key player in making this happen. After several trips to Washington, DC, we came up with a mockup of a circular table. It was a somewhat scientific experiment in ensuring the arc of the table did not obstruct anyone's line of sight. When all was said and done, it was a masterpiece, but albeit a bit larger than we had envisioned. The architects looked at the design specs and said that the table would not fit in the proposed boardroom and that it would make the hallway or the waiting area outside the room smaller. This, in my view, represented a convoluted sense of priorities. The architects seem to be saying that the size of the waiting area was apparently more important than communication access for deaf people. They also told us it would upset the aesthetics of the hall leading to the boardroom, making it look like the boardroom jutted into the hallway.

I stood my ground, and today, the room is as useful as it can be—in perpetuity!

GALLAUDET'S ENDOWMENT

When King assumed the presidency in 1988, some of the hearing people on the board, as well as many stakeholders, doubted whether a deaf president would be able to go before foundations and other organizations to raise the funds necessary to meet all of Gallaudet's financial needs. These funds would allow Gallaudet to afford new initiatives and programs that would not be possible if it had to rely on the support of the Federal government alone. King's success proved them all wrong. In 1988, Gallaudet's endowment stood at $8 million. At the time I stepped down from the board in 2001, the endowment had increased to $150 million. In a span of thirteen years, the endowment grew some $142 million, thanks to the fundraising prowess of King and investments in the stock market, not to mention the stewardship of the board's committee on resources and Paul Kelly, Gallaudet's chief financial officer.[9]

While King was busy raising funds, Phil Sprinkle, the chair of the Committee on Resources, was tasked to develop a methodology for managing our investments. He was an astute financial manager, even though he was a medical doctor, and I had the good fortune of observing him work with our investment advisors. He restructured our holdings to grow and exceed the various indexes of the financial markets by which we gauged

---

9. David F. Armstrong, "Deaf President Now and the Struggle for Deaf Control of Gallaudet University," *Sign Language Studies* 15, no. 1 (2014): 49–50.

the performance of our investments. After I stepped down as chair of the board in 1993, I chaired the Committee on Resources and followed Phil Sprinkle's methodology, which had served us so well.

CHANGES IN WASHINGTON, DC

In the Washington, DC, area, Gallaudet gained much name recognition. Before DPN, telling a taxi driver you were going to Gallaudet would be greeted with a blank stare. Only by adding the address would the taxi driver have some sense of where to go. After DPN, the stare was replaced by a knowing nod. One of the other ripple effects of DPN was the designation of the new Washington, DC, Metro station near Gallaudet as "New York Ave-Florida Ave-Gallaudet U" (it was rechristened as "NoMa-Gallaudet" in 2012). The addition of that station on the Red Line was the result of several years of effort by I. King Jordan, businesses in the vicinity, the DC government, and the DC Metro Board. This station has since triggered real estate development of the area around Gallaudet, and new businesses employ Gallaudet students and graduates.

FINAL THOUGHTS, LOOKING BACK

> God made the world in seven days and we have changed it in seven days.[10]

> —Charles A. Giansanti, Professor,
> Gallaudet University

This brings us to the end of my telling of the events of DPN and the impact of the movement. As I look back thirty-two years, I see that the deaf community today is, in many ways, a different community from what it was in 1988. We now have

---

10. Jack R. Gannon, *The Week the World Heard Gallaudet* (Washington, DC: Gallaudet University Press, 1989), 113.

deaf schools run by deaf people, with many middle managers (principals, supervising teachers) who are also deaf, working very well side by side with their hearing peers. We see many boards of schools and nonprofit organizations serving the deaf with a majority of deaf trustees. We see many more deaf lawyers and certified public accountants. We see more deaf entrepreneurs running web design companies and owning restaurants that serve the general population coffee, crepes, and pizzas. We see a deaf person walking home with the mirror trophy from the TV show, *Dancing with the Stars*. Some of the video relay companies and telecommunication companies are staffed with deaf executives. Deaf people are moving into executive positions in the government and Fortune 500 companies. We see deaf-owned technology companies and services, like ASL interpreting, closed captioning of television and movies, and video relay services, that are connecting us to the rest of the world.

All of these were unthinkable in 1988—the mere paradigm shift of being able to control our destiny has empowered us as deaf people to say, "Yes, we can!"

1988 was a perfect storm of elements that resulted in the success of the DPN movement. Hearing members of the Gallaudet University Board of Trustees completely misread the situation on campus. While perhaps unintentional, they denied the capabilities of deaf people, which oppressed the very group they were selected to serve. This was typical of how the hearing community (the majority) looked on us and, in the process, limited our opportunities as deaf people to grow and assert our identity as a community. At the same time, the deaf community was more educated than at any other time, and ASL and the cultural definition of deafness were becoming formalized, backed by research. All these factors were emerging at about the same time—they just needed a trigger, and the evening of March 7, 1988, was the spark that began our "Selma." Congressman David Bonior summed this up perfectly in 1998 at the teleconference, "The Pulse of the People: Ten Years After the Revolution."

It was the pulse of the people, ten very short years ago, that changed the way the world viewed Gallaudet University and the way deaf and hard of hearing people viewed themselves. When students, faculty, staff, and friends of Gallaudet stood symbolically, peacefully, and uniformly chanting, "Deaf President Now," the public saw those chants every day on TV, in the newspapers not just in Washington but around the country. . . .

And I remember thinking to myself, "This is the Deaf Selma; There's no turning back." Like many great movements in American history, the Gallaudet protest and the march of 1988 was a turning point. The Deaf community looked to Gallaudet for leadership, for inspiration, for hope, and for innovation. Shortly after the Deaf President Now, Congress passed the Americans with Disabilities Act which permanently altered the structure of American business. Together, these two great events enveloped the nation and bolstered the phrase that is often quoted by President Jordan, "Deaf people can do anything, except hear."[11]

I watched the movie *Selma* on a flight home about the time I was finishing up this book. I felt at peace after watching the movie. *We have arrived,* I thought to myself, *but the work will never be completed. We must continue to be vigilant . . . we have our inalienable rights endowed by our forefathers, and never again shall they be abridged!*

11. "In Their Own Words." Deaf President Now—Profiles and Viewpoints—In Their Words. Gallaudet University, accessed February 2, 2020, https://www.gallaudet.edu/about/history-and-traditions/deaf-president-now/profiles-and-viewpoints/in-their-own-words.

SUPPLEMENTAL MATERIALS

Notable Quotes about DPN

"DPN . . . was individuals standing up and saying, 'I do not, we do not, accept degraded status—yes, we require—that others accept this in us as well.'"[1]

—Roger Wilkins, Pulitzer–Prize–winning journalist and longtime advocate for the rights of black people in the United States and South Africa, in his 1993 commencement address at Gallaudet University.

"Seldom have I ever seen a civil rights movement so absolutely complete."[2]

—Senator Alan Cranston

"The 1988 protest by deaf students at Gallaudet University was a defining moment for the disability rights movement. It was the closest the movement has come to having a touchstone event, a Selma or a Stonewall. . . . The uprising that followed resonated for people of all disabilities, who empathized with the students' revolt against the paternalistic care of well-meaning but insensitive people who were not disabled. Gallaudet gave Americans a new rights consciousness about disability."[3]

—Joseph Shapiro

1. Gallaudet University, "Deaf President Now," accessed February 2, 2020, https://www.gallaudet.edu/about/history-and-traditions/deafpresident-now.

2. Gallaudet University, "Deaf President Now."

3. Joseph P. Shapiro, *No Pity: People with Disabilities Forging a New Civil Rights Movement* (New York: Times Books, 1994), 74–75.

"Overnight, it seemed like the new awareness about the needs and abilities of deaf people produced remarkable results on Capitol Hill. Bills that had been sitting idle in congressional committees suddenly found their way to the floors of the House and Senate, where they were swiftly passed into law. Over the course of only a few months, a bill introduced by Senator Harkin to enhance the use of technology to assist people with disabilities, legislation to establish a National Institute on Deafness and Other Communication Disorders, and legislation to require wireline telephones to be hearing aid-compatible became statutory mandates."[4]

—Karen Peltz Strauss

"The story of the Gallaudet University presidential search has no villains—no black hats, no white hats. It's not that sort of tale. The story is closer to that of the blind men and the elephant, a story about differences in perspective: Things happened as they did simply because people had different perceptions of what would best serve the university."[5]

—Jana Dozier, associate editor, Association of Governing Boards of Universities and Colleges

"Trusteeship is after all, a voluntary, part-time duty. Yet it calls for the best qualities available in the human form. More than for time, the demand is for quality of attention, and for mutual confidence. With all the factors at play in the Gallaudet situation, the

4. Karen Peltz Strauss, *A New Civil Right: Telecommunications Equality for Deaf and Hard of Hearing Americans* (Washington, DC: Gallaudet University Press, 2006), 66–67.

5. Jana Dozier, "Hear No Evil," *AGB Reports* 30, no. 4 (July/August 1988): 6–18.

new president faces a formidable task, as does the new board chair. Serious damage has been done. Any sense of victory among the prevailing group should be tempered by recognizing some other goals yet to be reached."[6]

> —J. L. Zwingle, president emeritus, Association of Governing Boards of Universities and Colleges

"When I had visited Gallaudet in 1986 and 1987, I found it an astonishing and moving experience. I had never before seen an entire community of the deaf, nor had I quite realized (even though I knew this theoretically) that Sign might indeed be a complete language—a language equally suitable for making love or speeches, for flirtation or mathematics."[7]

> —Oliver Sacks

"The most remarkable thing I've ever seen . . . If you'd asked me a month ago, I'd have bet a million dollars this couldn't happen in my lifetime. You've got to come down and see for yourself."[8]

> —Gallaudet Professor Bob Johnson to Oliver Sacks

"All sorts of changes, administrative, educational, social, psychological, are already beginning at Gallaudet. But what is clearest at this point is the much-altered bearing of its students, a bearing that conveys a new, wholly

6. J. L. Zwingle, "What Boards Can Learn from Gallaudet's Leadership Crisis," *AGB Reports* 30, no. 4 (July/August 1988): 14–15.

7. Oliver Sacks, *Seeing Voices: A Journey into the World of the Deaf* (Berkeley, CA: University of California Press, 1989), 127.

8. Oliver Sacks, "The Revolution of the Deaf," *New York Review of Books* 35, no. 9 (June 2, 1988): 23.

unselfconscious sense of pleasure and vindication, of confidence and dignity. This new sense of themselves represents a decisive break from the past, which could not have been imagined just a few months ago. But has all been changed? Will there be a lasting 'transformation of consciousness'? Will deaf people at Gallaudet, and the deaf community at large, indeed find the opportunities they seek? Will we, the hearing, allow them these opportunities? Allow them to be themselves, a unique culture in our midst, yet admit them as coequals, to every sphere of activity? One hopes the events at Gallaudet will be but the beginning."[9]

—Oliver Sacks

"Our anger, our years of repression, our disbelief, and our unity seemed to propel us forward with a velocity that surprised us all."[10]

—Jack Levesque

"We are grateful for Jack Levesque's columns on Gallaudet. Some of us were afraid, we were on the fence. But Jack came out and said it in 'Jack's Corner.' And we want to thank him. He was right. We thank him for being courageous, he was one of the very few who yelled loud. I wasn't yelling loud enough until I read his articles. Now Jack's one of our heroes. The faculty of Gallaudet are, too. Without their support, I don't think the students would have been successful."[11]

—Bill Ash

9. Oliver Sacks, *Seeing Voices: A Journey into the World of the Deaf* (Berkeley, CA: University of California Press, 1989), 159.

10. Jack Levesque, "WOW! What a Ride!" *DCARA News*, April 1988.

11. Bill Ash, "Who Said What When . . . In Their Own Words," *DCARA News*, April 1988.

"I thank Providence for all that happened in March. It means a great deal to me to have your good wishes, and I can tell you that from my earliest days at Gallaudet, it was my deep conviction that people like me should move over as soon possible, so that Deaf people could take our places and the pinnacle of Deaf education reflect the wisdom of the Deaf community. I am delighted that it happened in my lifetime. The Board couldn't have picked a better executive for the new enterprise than King nor found a better Chairman. There are usually serious upheavals after a successful revolution, but as long as you and King and the Board insist that the institution puts quality education for deaf persons uppermost, all will be well."[12]

—Dr. Bill Stokoe

"Perhaps the greatest moment in the history of this university occurred in 1988 when the community came together and said, 'We will no longer accept the judgment of others about our lives and leadership in this university; these are our responsibilities, and we accept the challenge.' In days, what was known as the 'Deaf President Now' movement changed the way our entire country looks at deaf people. The Nation watched as you organized and built a movement of conscience unlike any other. You removed barriers of limited expectations, and our Nation saw that deaf people can do anything hearing people can but hear."[13]

—President Bill Clinton at 1994
Commencement, Gallaudet University

12. Bill Stokoe, Letter from Bill Stokoe to Phil and Judy Bravin. From the private collection of Philip W. Bravin, September 1, 1988.

13. William J. Clinton, "Remarks at the Gallaudet University Commencement Ceremony," Commencement address, Gallaudet University, Washington, DC, 908, accessed May 13, 1994, https://www.govinfo.gov/content/pkg/PPP-1994-book1/pdf/PPP-1994-book1-doc-pg906.pdf.

"Since its charter was signed by President Abraham Lincoln 150 years ago, Gallaudet University has been a world leader in providing higher education that ensures the intellectual and professional advancement of deaf and hard-of-hearing individuals . . . the Deaf President Now movement at Gallaudet in 1988 provided critical momentum for the passage of the Americans with Disabilities Act two years later, and I know we could not have achieved that without many years of hard work and dedication from leaders and advocates like those at Gallaudet University."[14]

—Senator Tom Harkin, on the occasion of the 150th anniversary of Gallaudet University

14. Tom Harkin, "Harkin Statement on 150th Anniversary of Gallaudet University: The US Senate Committee on Health, Education, Labor & Pensions, accessed April 8, 2014, https://www.help.senate.gov/ranking/newsroom/press/harkin-statement-on-150th-anniversary-of-gallaudet-university.

Controlling Our Destiny:
An Unpublished Paper

While I was going through my papers to prepare for writing this book, I found the following essay. I wrote it two-and-a-half years after the DPN movement. Thirty years later, we are still seeing the pockets of oppression that I outlined in this paper. I titled it "Controlling Our Destiny," but I do not have any recollection as to whether it was published or was something I wrote one night on the spur of the moment due to some development.

Since the Deaf President Now movement in 1988, winds of change have blown throughout the deaf community, both in the United States and abroad. The basic right of deaf people to control their destiny was the basic issue of that movement. Since then, we have begun to see deaf people being appointed to head schools for the deaf. There has been a corresponding movement in appointing deaf people to boards of such schools, but at a much slower pace than we all would like to see. Very few boards in this country have a deaf majority. The Gallaudet University Board of Trustees, which I chair, has declared its intent to achieve this, and they are working toward this very achievable goal.

Why am writing this? In the past two-and-a-half years, even though change has happened, it is still meeting with some interesting resistance from certain quarters, especially from boards of privately run but state-supported schools for the deaf. In addition, a majority of deaf children in this country are educated in mainstreamed programs. We have yet to see boards of education in various parts of this country reaching into the deaf community to seek input and representation to educate deaf children. Some state-supported schools do not have a board of trustees (an operating one, per se) but instead have an advisory board with varying degrees of clout. These boards also have very limited representation of deaf people.

If deaf people are not represented on boards of such institutions, how can we ensure that our deaf children in this country are assured that they are provided with the best education possible? We have seen enough shortcomings in the educational system when it comes to educating deaf children, merely because such decisions are made by people who very often have little, if any, appreciation and understanding of the basic requirements of a deaf child, which are uniquely different from their hearing peers.

Let us put ourselves to task—make a very sincere effort in placing deaf people on boards of schools for the deaf in this country, assuring that boards of education in various communities have some form of representation from the deaf community to provide substantial (not token) input to the educational process of deaf children. The ultimate goal, of course, is to eventually insure that every program of, by, and for deaf people has a governing or advisory board (where this has to be the case) that is composed of a majority of deaf people, both from within the community it serves as well as national or statewide leaders. This way, we will then have begun to control our destiny because we will be in control of a process that creates a productive deaf citizen of this country.

Let us all work toward this goal!

Cast of Characters

Dave Bonior: Congressman from Michigan (Democrat). Bonior became a professor of labor studies at Wayne State University, and he founded the American Rights at Work, a union advocacy organization. He has also become a restaurateur, owning and operating the restaurants Agua 301 and Zest.

Philip Bravin: Deaf community leader and IBM product administrator (currently, a vice president at ZVRS/Purple, a video relay company).

Dr. Harvey J. Corson: Deaf superintendent of the Louisiana School for the Deaf—stepped down from the board temporarily while a candidate for the presidency. (Retired)

Jean McDermott Crabtree: Community member and wife of an otolaryngologist from California. (Retired)

Dr. Laurel Glass: Medical doctor and researcher in the field of late-onset deafness and mental health at the University of California. (Deceased)

Steve Gunderson: Congressman from Wisconsin (Republican). Currently CEO of the Career Education Colleges and Universities.

Charles Haskell: Publisher of the *Mt. Sterling Advocate*, a newspaper in Kentucky. (Deceased)

Dr. Jim Hicks: Medical doctor, otolaryngologist, and gentleman farmer from Alabama. (Deceased)

Senator Daniel K. Inouye: A US senator (Democrat) from Hawaii from 1963 until his death in 2012. He was president pro tempore of the United States Senate from 2010 until his death. (Deceased)

Judge Thomas Penfield Jackson: A federal district judge in Washington, DC. (Deceased)

Jay Parker. A community leader in Washington, DC, and founder and president of the Lincoln Institute for Research and Education. (Deceased)

Alexander Patterson Jr.: Former GTE and IBM executive from Connecticut. (Deceased)

Gustave Rathe: Former IBM executive from Louisiana, New Mexico, California, and Virginia. (Deceased)

Vincent Reed: Vice president of communications at the *Washington Post*, former superintendent of schools in Washington, DC, and assistant US secretary of education. (Retired)

Robert Sanderson: Deaf community leader from Utah. (Deceased)

Jane Bassett Spilman: Furniture magnate—Bassett Furniture from Bassett, Virginia, currently living outside Richmond, Virginia. (Retired)

Dr. Phil Sprinkle: Medical doctor, otolaryngologist, and astute financial investor from West Virginia. (Deceased)

Frank B. Sullivan: Deaf community leader from Illinois and Maryland. (Deceased)

Eloise Thornberry: Wife of US Senator Homer Thornberry from Texas. (Deceased)

THE FOUR STUDENT LEADERS (CURRENT POSITIONS)

Jerry Covell: Currently, director of the Illinois Commission for the Deaf and Hard of Hearing.

Bridgetta Bourne-Firl: Currently, director of outreach services at the Laurent Clerc National Center on the Gallaudet campus.

Greg Hlibok: Currently, chief legal officer at ZVRS/Purple, a video relay company (formerly chief of the Disability Rights Office at the Federal Communications Commission).

Tim Rarus: Currently, a vice president at ZVRS/Purple, a video relay company.

PHIL'S FAITHFUL RIGHT-HAND PERSON

Lillian Holt: Chief of staff for the provost at Gallaudet. (Retired)

THE EIGHTH PRESIDENT OF GALLAUDET

I. King Jordan: Currently serves on several boards all over the country, often called upon to speak as a disability rights advocate. (Retired)

Deaf President Now! A Ballad
by Robert F. Panara

Gallaudet University celebrated the fifth anniversary of Deaf President Now (DPN) at a black-tie gala at the Westin Hotel in Washington, DC, on October 25, 1993. Dr. Robert F. Panara, a member of the Class of 1945, wrote the following ballad for this event, and it was performed by the well-known deaf actor, Bernard Bragg, a member of the Class of 1952. The author appreciates the gesture of the Panara family who gave permission to print this ballad. It was originally published in the December 1991 issue of the Gallaudet Alumni Newsletter.

Deaf President Now!

The vote was cast at Gallaudet
And shattered every dream—
"Deaf people are not ready yet
To rule in academe."

The students soon rose up in arms
With reason to complain
And cried, "The Chairman of the Board
Has caused this day of shame!

"They chose a hearing president Who
does not even Sign,
Not one we asked to represent us—
A man of our own kind."

So, in protest, they closed their ranks
And formed a barricade
To block the Board from trespassing
Their campus-wide crusade.

They chose four student leaders
To represent their bloc—
Tim Rarus, Jerry Covell,
Bridgetta Bourne, and Greg Hlibok.

The foursome voiced their joint concerns
Of all that was unfair,
And made their Deaf Identity
A common cause to share.

They said, "As history has shown
Throughout a hundred years,
Deaf people still can hold their own
When matched with hearing peers.

"The Board has heard this quote before—
A truth that's very clear—
It isn't what you use them for
But what's between the ears!

"We want to shape the destiny
Of those who come to learn
At this great University
Where Sign is our concern,

"Where hands are used to make the words
For eyes to understand
And, just as worthy, Youth is served
To lead and to command.

"Yes, now it's time to draw the line
And we will show them how
In unison our hands will sign—
We Want DEAF PRESIDENT NOW!

"Our buttons shall read DPN,
Which means DEAF PRESIDENT NOW!
It only takes three words to sign
Our Cause—DEAF PRESIDENT NOW!"

And soon five thousand tramping feet
Begin their great parade,
As "DPN" their hands repeat
The cause of their crusade.

Their ranks are swelled as thousands pour
To Washington, DC
The scene where twenty million more
Are watching on TV.

Where deaf and hearing join as one
In justice to avow:
"For Gallaudet, the time has come—
We Want DEAF PRESIDENT NOW!"

VOTE DPN! VOTE DPN!
The message went around
The Board was forced to meet again
To heed the sight and sound.

The Chairman of the Board resigned;
The President-elect
Had reconsidered and declined
(And did so with respect).

The balloting began again,
And when the votes were in,
They tallied up a DPN
And a smashing student win!

And, by this act, a precedent
Was subsequently set—
The new Chairman and the President
Were schooled at Gallaudet.

They presented I. King Jordan,
A man so aptly named,
Who stood tall and proud before them
As they drowned him with acclaim.

As I. King Jordan took the stage
To greet his student fans
Wave after wave of "DPN"
Erupted from their hands!

He said: "If we have learned one thing,
Its truth is very clear—
DEAF PEOPLE CAN DO ANYTHING,
YES, ANYTHING BUT HEAR!

"I accept your acclamation
And I'll do my best to be
The first deaf President to run
Our university."

L'Envoi

Four weary students rolled their eyes
And marveled, "Holy Cow!
Can you believe what we achieved—
We have DEAF PRESIDENT NOW!"

You Have to Be Deaf to Understand
by Willard J. Madsen[15]

What is it like to "hear" a hand?
You have to be deaf to understand.

What is it like to be a small child,
In a school, in a room void of sound—
With a teacher who talks and talks and talks;
And then when she does come around to you,
She expects you to know what she's said?
You have to be deaf to understand.

Or the teacher thinks that to make you smart,
You must first learn how to talk with your voice;
So mumbo-jumbo with hands on your face
For hours and hours without patience or end,
Until out comes a faint resembling sound?
You have to be deaf to understand.

What is it like to be curious,
To thirst for knowledge you can call your own,
With an inner desire that's set on fire—
And you ask a brother, sister, or friend
Who looks in answer and says, "Never mind"?
You have to be deaf to understand.

What it is like in a corner to stand,
Though there's nothing you've done really wrong,
Other than try to make use of your hands
To a silent peer to communicate

15. Jack R. Gannon, *Deaf Heritage: A Narrative History of Deaf America* (Washington, DC: Gallaudet University Press, 2012), 380.

A thought that comes to your mind all at once?
You have to be deaf to understand.

What is it like to be shouted at
When one thinks that will help you to hear;
Or misunderstand the words of a friend
Who is trying to make a joke clear,
And you don't get the point because he's failed?
You have to be deaf to understand.

What is it like to be laughed in the face
When you try to repeat what is said;
Just to make sure that you've understood,
And you find that the words were misread—
And you want to cry out, "Please help me, friend"?
You have to be deaf to understand.

What is it like to have to depend
Upon one who can hear to phone a friend;
Or place a call to a business firm
And be forced to share what's personal, and,
Then find that your message wasn't made clear?
You have to be deaf to understand.

What is it like to be deaf and alone
In the company of those who can hear—
And you only guess as you go along,
For no one's there with a helping hand,
As you try to keep up with words and song?
You have to be deaf to understand.

What is it like on the road of life
To meet with a stranger who opens his mouth—
And speaks out a line at a rapid pace;
And you can't understand the look in his face

Because it is new and you're lost in the race?
You have to be deaf to understand.

What is it like to comprehend
Some nimble fingers that paint the scene,
And make you smile and feel serene
With the "spoken word" of the moving hand
That makes you part of the world at large?
You have to be deaf to understand.

What is it like to "hear" a hand?
Yes, you have to be deaf to understand.

The Dr. Edward C. Merrill Jr. Papers

The following four documents (two letters and two papers) were uncovered by the author in his research for this book. The Merrill family generously gave the author permission to reprint those documents in their entirety; they have not been published or seen anywhere in the public domain until now. Altogether, these documents provide the foresight of Gallaudet's fourth president on the untapped capabilities of deaf people to take their rightful place in society by starting to control their destiny. In hindsight, Dr. Merrill was one of the few hearing people who had the perception that many of his hearing colleagues missed or didn't have. The author is eternally grateful for the opportunity to share these documents for posterity.

LETTER FROM DR. EDWARD C. MERRILL JR.
TO GEORGE MUTH[16]

Gallaudet College
Washington, DC 20002

Office of the President

July 15, 1982

Mr. George E. Muth
Chairman
Board of Trustees
Gallaudet College
800 Florida Ave., NE
Washington, DC 20002

Dear Mr. Muth:

Attached to this letter you will find a paper entitled, "Challenges Facing the Fifth President of Gallaudet College." This paper represents my efforts to describe my own perception of the challenges which will face the next president of Gallaudet College for perhaps five to eight years. The paper has two distinct limitations: as the incumbent president, I am sure there are tasks which I do not perceive. Furthermore, I am writing this paper a full year before the next president will take office. It is quite possible that additional tasks will arise between now and then. In any event, I trust this paper will be useful to members of the Board of Trustees

---

16. Edward C. Merrill, Letter from Dr. Edward C. Merrill Jr. to George Muth, July 15, 1982. Courtesy of the author's personal files (reprinted with permission from the Merrill family).

and advisory committees involved in the search for the next president. I should hope that it would suggest the kinds of strengths which will be needed to provide leadership for Gallaudet College in the future.

I have also written a paper entitled, "The Feasibility of a Deaf Person as President of Gallaudet College." Although I agreed to write and to present such a paper to the Board of Trustees, I should like to request your permission to withhold this paper. The issue of a deaf person serving as president of Gallaudet College is actually moot. The College has a very strong Affirmative Action commitment which indicates that persons are eligible for any position in the institution regardless of handicapping condition. Beyond this, we have deaf persons currently holding responsible management positions (Vice Presidents, Deans, Directors), and their performance in these positions is indistinguishable from hearing persons who hold similar positions. The evidence on ability of deaf persons as administrators is already in and there is little more to say. A deaf person who is qualified has every right to hold the position and can reasonably be expected to do as well as a hearing person. Deafness, therefore, is no basis for questioning a qualified candidate, nor is it a basis which unduly recommends him.

Although I have no further comment on the feasibility of a deaf person as president, I should like to bring to your attention the fact that deafness would be an asset to an individual serving as the fifth president of Gallaudet College in at least three ways: first, a deaf person serving as president would be seen as representative of the mission of the institution. He could speak both for deaf people and the College and would automatically have a level of credibility which could hardly be attained by a hearing person. Second, I think that a deaf person serving as president would be quite attractive to students who may aspire to attend Gallaudet College. Not only would students identify with him and have great confidence in his administration, but he would obviously be able to communicate quite clearly with them. Finally, a deaf president even though he were not an alumnus of the institution, would obviously be a symbol of the success of education of deaf persons in this nation. After 118 years of educational effort, it would be timely, indeed, if a deaf person could assume the presidency of an institution of higher learning.

With your permission, I will let the remarks above stand in lieu of the paper which I have written about an issue which really needs no further comment.

Sincerely yours,
Edward C. Merrill Jr.

THE FEASIBILITY OF A DEAF PERSON SERVING AS PRESIDENT OF GALLAUDET COLLEGE[17]

Edward C. Merrill Jr.[18]

Any individual, organization, agency, or institution which endeavors to assist disabled people must face a very penetrating, basic question. The answer to this question is for whoever formulates it a "moment of truth." The question is this: No matter how noble, eleemosynary, or effective the individual or organization is, is the individual or organization really benefiting the disabled person or is the individual in society benefiting more by providing these programs and services? Obviously many of our professional people and the programs they offered have benefited deaf people. It is equally clear that these professionals have found rewarding careers and the institutions they represented have found substantial and public recognition.

Why would a question of this nature be raised in a paper focusing on the feasibility of a deaf person as the fifth president of Gallaudet College? It is raised deliberately as a philosophical frame of reference within which one can see clearly the very fundamental basis of credibility which a deaf person would have as the chief executive officer of Gallaudet College. A deaf president would have a degree of credibility which can never be obtained by a hearing person because the deaf individual would, himself, possess the disability on which the mission of the institution is focused and presumably he would have also overcome this disability to a substantial extent.

---

17. Edward C. Merrill, "The Feasibility of a Deaf Person Serving as President of Gallaudet College," July 7, 1982, unpublished ms. From the private collection of Philip W. Bravin (reprinted with permission from the Merrill family).

18. This is an opinion paper developed by Edward C. Merrill Jr., president, Gallaudet College, Washington, DC (July 1982). This paper is developed for the Board of Trustees of Gallaudet College as they search for the fifth president of Gallaudet College, whose term of office will begin on October 1, 1983.

This brief philosophical discourse leads me to a position from which I think the feasibility of a deaf person serving as president of Gallaudet College can be viewed, a position which would be as follows: deafness, per se, is no basis for disqualifying a candidate for the presidency of Gallaudet College; furthermore, deafness offers an unprecedented opportunity to establish the credibility of the institution in an unquestionable manner, provided this person is qualified to perform the office in a competent manner.

With this position in mind, I should like to comment on how a deaf president might respond to the demands of this office state in a companion paper entitled, "Challenges Facing the Fifth President of Gallaudet College." This paper discusses the major tasks which will face the next president of Gallaudet College during the next five to eight years.

I. Mission

A deaf president would have not only penetrating insights into the mission of Gallaudet College, but a deeper appreciation of it. Regardless of whether the deaf president was a graduate of Gallaudet College or not, he would also be in a position to be more critical of the manner in which the institution is responding to its mission and he would obviously be in a position to extend this mission to needs he has felt. I should hasten to add, however, that I feel that deafness, per se, is no guarantee of inventiveness or creativity in the formulation and establishment of educational goals. In summary, the deaf candidate would have an appreciation of the mission of Gallaudet College and tremendous credibility in projecting this mission. If he had in addition creativity and genuine inventiveness in continuing the evolution of this mission in relation to the changing needs of deaf people or of knowing how to do this with the assistance of his associates, he would be a tremendous and successful leader for the college.

II. Resources

How would a deaf president respond to the pressing challenge of increasing federal funding and also financial support from the private sector for Gallaudet College?

In developing budgets, the president of Gallaudet College largely depends upon staff assistance. In presenting budgets to the Department of Education, OMB,[19] the congressional committees, the president is the key spokesman for the institution. In these settings, I think a deaf president could bring unprecedented credibility to the defense of budget requests. He would have to be sure that he could be understood clearly and that he could respond appropriately. I think the deaf president could provide responses which had great authenticity provided his communication skills permitted him to be adequately fluent and clearly understood.

The same condition would exist in meeting with foundation and corporate officials. In other words, a deaf president could present the case of Gallaudet College in a more credible manner than a hearing person could ever do and he could also present it free from any suspicion that he might be exploiting the disability of other people. He would encounter initial concerns that persons unfamiliar with deaf people normally feel. These can be rapidly overcome by clear communication. Once this is done the deaf person would have a decided advantage in seeking financial support from the private sector in my opinion, for he would not be talking about the need but he would be illustrating the impact of deafness on an individual. He would also be demonstrating the benefit of the educational programs which he had obtained.

III. Students

Although there is no assurance that deafness brings with it an automatic interest or affection toward young people, any deaf person who were named to the office of president of Gallaudet

---

19. OMB refers to the Office of Management and Budget.

College would logically have been an individual who has demonstrated his interests in deaf youth. Other than this it is obvious that a deaf president would have the respect and admiration of deaf young people. He would be inevitably an inspiration to them and a source of pride that a person who shared their disability could have achieved so well. Although Gallaudet College is struggling to accept an increased enrollment for the next three or four years, after that the presence of a deaf president could be a critically important factor in the continued interest of young deaf people in attending this institution.

IV. Faculty

The assumption would be that any person selected as president of Gallaudet College would have respectable academic credentials. Inasmuch as deaf persons have increasing access to advanced degree programs, it is reasonable to expect deaf candidates who have appropriate academic credentials. In my opinion, it would be a mistake to name a person as president of Gallaudet college who was deaf but who did not have appropriate academic credentials. This would tend to develop unnecessary stress between the administration and the faculty and have still other damaging implications concerning the overall academic quality of the institution.

V. Advocacy

Although Gallaudet College has evolved during the past few years as a strong advocate for deaf persons, a deaf president would, in my opinion, become a strong national and international advocate. His credibility would be unquestionable and I would predict that he could become a major spokesman for deaf people as well as the institution. Depending to some degree on his personality, his style, and his communication skills, a deaf president could emerge as a leader of tremendous proportions. As such, he could bring recognition to Gallaudet College which it has never had before.

VI. Public Awareness

As with advocacy, a deaf president could become nationally and internationally known. If this were to occur, he could achieve vast improvements in public awareness of deafness and deaf people. This would particularly occur if the individual became nationally recognized and a "national figure." Much would be determined on the individual's personality and style as suggested above. If he had a dynamic personality and the ability to manage communication so that his message was both clear and interesting to the general public, he could make a tremendous contribution toward the understanding of this disability and its acceptance in the general society. This, however, is only a possibility. A hearing person with saleable and appealing public relation skills can go far as the president of Gallaudet College—but never as far as a person who has these same skills and is representative of an individual who has largely overcome this disability.

VII. Management

The internal management of Gallaudet College has increased substantially as the College has grown in the number of persons served, the number of programs offered, assumed a more complex structure, and required a larger budget. It would be critical for a deaf president to have had direct management responsibility and experience. Experience in higher education would be valuable but management experience in another organization would probably be equally valid. The traditions of higher education, in particular faculty governance, are important and require considerable sensitivity on the part of the president, but these specialized administrative arrangements can be learned.

The chief administrative officer of any college or university must have the ability to structure the internal operation of the institution so that units function reasonably well without daily management and so that tasks can be delegated. In my opinion deafness provides no insurmountable barrier to the management of a college or university, particularly Gallaudet College. We already have a very valuable track record of deaf vice presidents, deans, and directors who were both men and women as well as minority groups here at Gallaudet College. The Board of Trustees would need to know that the deaf candidate had adequate management skills including general attractiveness and interest in the wide range of employees of Gallaudet College. Once determined, the challenges in this area would seem to be easily performed by a qualified deaf individual.

VIII. Summary

With apologies for the length of this paper, I am pleased to present this analysis of the feasibility of a deaf person serving as the firth president of Gallaudet College. Any deaf candidate should meet the qualification of the office. Any deaf candidates should demonstrate the potential for becoming a genuine leader, not only in projecting the mission of the institution and finding resources to support it but in the profession and in higher education. Having these qualities, deafness offers advantages of obtaining higher levels of credibility in the office of president and for the institution which can be obtained in no other way. Furthermore, deafness presents no barrier which I can identify that would, per se, prevent a candidate with other talents and abilities to perform this position well. As a matter of fact, were the fifth president of Gallaudet College to be deaf, he would be a living expression of the importance and value of educational opportunity for deaf people everywhere.

Draft - 7/7/82 ECM,Jr./gf

7-7-82

Do Not Distribute

THE FEASIBILITY OF A DEAF PERSON
SERVING AS PRESIDENT OF GALLAUDET COLLEGE

by

Edward C. Merrill, Jr.[1]

File

Any individual, organization, agency, or institution which endeavors to assist disabled people must face a very penetrating, basic question. The answer to this question is for whoever formulates it a "moment of truth." The question is this: No matter how noble, eleemosynary, or effective the individual or organization is, is the individual or organization really benefiting the disabled person or is the individual in society benefiting more by providing these programs and services? Obviously many of our professional people and the programs they offered have benefited deaf people. It is equally clear that these professionals have found rewarding careers and the institutions they represented have found substantial support and public recognition.

Why would a question of this nature be raised in a paper focusing on the feasibility of a deaf person as the fifth president of Gallaudet College? It is raised deliberately as a philosophical frame of reference within which one can see clearly the very fundamental basis of credibility which a deaf person would have as the chief executive officer of Gallaudet College. A deaf president would have a degree of credibility which can never be obtained by a hearing person because the deaf individual would, himself, possess the disability on which the mission of the institution is focused and presumably he would have also overcome this disability to a substantial extent.

[1]This is an opinion paper developed by Edward C. Merrill, Jr., President, Gallaudet College, Washington, D. C. (July 1982). This paper is developed for the Board of Trustees of Gallaudet College as they search for the fifth president of Gallaudet College whose term of office will begin October 1, 1983

This is the cover page of the Merrill paper on "The Feasibility of a Deaf Person Serving as President of Gallaudet College." The family verified the handwriting as Dr. Merrill's.

CHALLENGES FACING THE FIFTH PRESIDENT OF GALLAUDET COLLEGE[20]

Edward C. Merrill Jr. [21]

Gallaudet College, as an accredited multipurpose institution of higher education, is much like other colleges in the United States in its goals, curricula, structure, faculty, management, physical plant and financial needs, outreach, and even its student body. On the other hand, Gallaudet College is quite unique inasmuch as it is an institution whose mission is focused on meeting the academic and intellectual needs of deaf people throughout the nation. It is also unique as a federally sponsored independent college under the direction of a self-perpetuating Board of Trustees with the exception of those members of the Board who are Congressional representatives. So Gallaudet College is more similar to other colleges in the spectrum of higher education in the United States than it is different; however, the differences are critical ones which must always be kept foremost in the mind or the institution loses a great deal of its meaning and character.

No one can foretell the future of a college or university, for much of the future of any institution of higher education is dependent upon those factors over which it has no control. An institution of higher education is first of all dependent upon the interest and desire of young people to see an education there and to pursue its degree programs. It is dependent upon a vast network of support from alumni, faculty, friends of the college, and in the case of Gallaudet College, the federal government. At the same time, the College has a mission which is

---

20. Edward C. Merrill, "Challenges Facing the Fifth President of Gallaudet College," August 1982. Paper. From the private collection of Philip W. Bravin (reprinted with permission from the Merrill family).

21. This is an opinion paper developed by Edward C. Merrill Jr., president, Gallaudet College, Washington, DC (July 1982). The paper is developed for the board of trustees of Gallaudet College as they search for the fifth president of Gallaudet College whose term of office will begin on October 1, 1983.

not only reflected in a set of very valuable purposes, but which is also recognized by the federal government and public nationally and internationally.

Although no one knows what the future holds, it is possible to project some of the critical, continuing needs of the institution which will be very much in the mind and heart of the fifth president of this institution. Even though the fifth president of this institution will respond to the leadership challenges of this institution in his own manner and with his own priorities, it may be useful to the Board of Trustees to have a perspective of what these challenges may be from the incumbent of his office. The purpose of this paper, therefore, is to present an overview of the challenges which appear, at least here and now, to be those which will face the new president even though they come from a very limited perspective.

I. Mission

The most vital and continuing challenges of the fifth president of Gallaudet College will be to define and to redefine for the Board of Trustees the continuing mission of Gallaudet College as the national college for deaf people. As the educational level of deaf programs rises, as attitudes toward higher education change, as new demands for intellectual acuity appear, as the academic and professional needs of deaf people change in order for them to lead productive and independent lives, as the kinds of professionals needed by deaf people also change, what efforts will be made for Gallaudet College to respond? The most vital characteristics of the fifth president of Gallaudet College will probably not be unlike the dominant characteristics of its first president, Dr. Edward Miner Gallaudet. It was he who saw the vast unmet academic and intellectual needs of deaf people and resolved to build an institution to meet them. The fifth president of Gallaudet College must also be perceptive and ingenious enough to know how to shape the mission of this institution so that it responds to these needs with a high degree of predictability and effectiveness. If the Gallaudet College of 1990 and 1995 and 2000 is not responsive to the academic and intellectual needs of deaf people throughout the nation in creative, varied, and effective ways, the college will very likely be a dying institution. The next president must redefine the mission of this institution periodically so that it continues to be in direct interaction with the client[ele] for whom it exists.

II. Resources

Gallaudet College is federally sponsored. This means that the college offers several academic programs at the elementary, secondary, and collegiate levels as well as research and public service programs which have strong authorizing federal legislation. There is evidence also that the United States Government, even in the midst of economic duress, will continue to honor its commitment to the institution; however, the evidence is also clear that this commitment is not apt to be expanded substantially.

One of the central challenges of the fifth president of Gallaudet College will be to establish and to maintain effective relationships with the Department of Education, the Office of Management and Budget, the subcommittees for appropriations of the House of Representative and the Senate. The federal government is responsive to the needs of handicapped people provided these needs can be described well, met by viable programs, have definitive results, and are reasonably cost-effective. The next president, therefore, must be able to put together a team of people who can work toward the end of maintaining and increasing federal financial support for Gallaudet College. This involves, of course, not only strong supporting staff people here, but the generation of grassroots support through the alumni, parents, and other organizations in various states. Congressmen generally respond positively to Gallaudet College when they are convinced that the programs and services of the institution are meaningful to constituencies within their respective states.

The fifth president of Gallaudet College must also seek financial support from the private sector. The mission of Gallaudet College is so vital and appealing to the general public that it is sad, indeed, that no breakthrough has occurred in obtaining broad private support from the donations for the cause which this college represents. To build financial support from the private sector will be a major challenge for the next president. The framework for this kind of support is taking shape. A direct mail campaign, annual giving, and support from the business sector should grow and provide increasing amounts of support. When the Gallaudet Educational Foundation to established, this should provide a vitally important sustained increases [*sic*] in the amount of nonfederal funds which are available periodically to support programs and services at the College.

In speaking about financial needs of the College, one must not overlook the fact that financial resources are obtained by and through people. Although the federal government is seen as a large, complicated bureaucracy, one relates to this organization through individuals who are serving in the various departments or in Congressional offices. It is important for the president to be able to be personable and have a high degree of credibility as he works with those individuals. This, of course, also applies to the private sector. Although we contact foundations, corporations, alumni, and friends of the College, the contacts with these groups occur with specific individuals.

The fifth president of Gallaudet College must be a fundraiser from both the federal and the private sectors. Although it is vital for the president of an institution to be accessible to and associate with students and faculty, the fifth president of Gallaudet College should plan to give from 30 percent to 50 percent of this time to developing the financial base of Gallaudet College. No matter how important the mission of an institution of higher education, it will not be achieved without adequate resources.

III. Students

This mission of Gallaudet College is first and foremost to provide education for children and students. Although we generally think of students as young people, Gallaudet offers adult basic and continuing education to increasing numbers of older people. For the past three years, moreover, Gallaudet College has been preparing to receive a surge of students. Children born during the rubella epidemic of 1964 and 1965 will become college age in 1983, 1984, and 1985. The College is challenged to serve this increased number of students. In all probability the physical facilities will be available to serve the first wave of these students as the fifth president takes office; however, the probability of obtaining adequate operational funds is much less sure. He will need to seek considerable additional funds to support the continued large enrollments which will result from serving the regular contingency of students plus those deafened during the rubella epidemic.

Although this may seem to indicate that the fifth president will not need to concern himself with declining student enrollments, the base of many colleges today, accommodating and sustaining student enrollments may not be done without some effort. Several developments indicate that the students who normally would increase the enrollment of Gallaudet College will encounter increasing difficulty in attending here. Some of the developments which will compromise the access of students to programs designed for them at Gallaudet are as follows: there is a prevailing attitude that mainstreaming is better even though there is considerable evidence that this does not work well for many hearing impaired students at the postsecondary level. Rehabilitation funds which have been important in financing students at Gallaudet College have been cut drastically, resulting in only limited support from this source. Other special programs have developed throughout the states, largely in community colleges. These attract students who wish to remain near home or pursue strictly technical courses although these programs may not be challenging or, for that matter, even accredited. In addition to all of this, various federal student loan programs have been drastically reduced. During and after the increased enrollments due to the rubella students, the fifth president of the Gallaudet College will need to be an effective representative of this institution with a high degree of credibility as he makes plans to keep hearing impaired young people informed of the advantages of attending Gallaudet College, of pursuing a more general degree, of preparing themselves for work and an independent life. The fifth president, therefore, must not only be interested in students, interesting to students, and individual of credibility with students, but he must also be able to assist students to understand what a college education can mean to them.

IV. Faculty

The faculty members of Gallaudet College are the heart of the institution. They are responsible for providing the instruction, the means by which students grow and develop during their four or five years at Gallaudet College. The next president of Gallaudet College should be academically respectable so that he is qualified as a faculty member. More than this, however, the president should have a very positive attitude toward pre-collegiate and collegiate facilities. He should recognize their vital role, be accessible to them, and see himself as, not apart from, but one of them even though he has heavy administrative responsibilities. He should understand faculty governance in higher education and actively seek faculty opinions through an organized approach.

V. Advocacy

The president of Gallaudet College, as one might expect, is seen as a spokesman for the institution. Iasmuch [sic] as Gallaudet College is the only college for the deaf in the world, what the president says or writes not only represents the college but also makes a statement about deafness or deaf people. It is not unusual to find great credence given to what the president of Gallaudet College say[s] here in the United States and in other countries as well. The substance of what the president of Gallaudet College says in various forums, the manner in which comments are made, and the attitude which they reflect toward deaf people are extremely important. The president of Gallaudet College must not only be a "true believer" in deaf people but he must also identify with them. This, of course, is a subtle characteristic, but it is essential if an individual is to have credibility with those persons with whom and for whom he works.

In addition to being an advocate himself, the president of Gallaudet College must orient the institution so that it is seen as an advocate for deaf people everywhere. This has been achieved to some degree during the present administration by having a very effective deaf person as Special Assistant to the President who is deaf himself. The fifth president of Gallaudet College must not only be totally acceptable to deaf people but he must be seen as an individual who can become an important advocate of the interest and welfare of deaf people. Although this characteristic argues strongly for a deaf candidate, the possibility of a hearing person performing this role as effectively, is not improbable, provided he is totally committed to deaf people.

VI. Public Awareness

The task of developing positive public awareness of deaf and the rights and abilities of deaf people is extremely difficult. It is difficult because of the nature of deafness, because of the competition of other special interest groups, because of the continuous need for publicity, and because of the limited opportunity for substantive discussion. Public awareness of deafness and public understanding of deafness are critical in order to generate support of special programs which are needed by deaf people and opportunities for employment. Although the next president of Gallaudet College has more important tasks listed above than to be a typical "P.R." person, he should have P.R. sensitivity, know-how and salability. Public awareness leads to broader understanding of deafness. This in turn leads to acceptance of deaf people and public support of programs and services for them—including Gallaudet College.

VII. Administration

For a new president, the internal management of the institution will constitute a challenge. Doubtless, he will want to consider a variety of changes and developments in policy, structure, and advice mechanisms. On the other hand, the existing officers and the structure for which they are responsible will permit significant delegation of a wide range of tasks and activities. As the administrative structure changes and evolves, he will probably be in a position to delegate still further responsibility and management duties. He will probably want to spend up to 50 percent of his time on external activities, especially those related to increasing financial and human resources of the institution. This category of challenges, i.e. management, is mentioned merely because it will necessitate time and attention although the tasks mentioned previously will be much more absorbing and require considerably more energy.

In concluding, it is hopeful that this view of the five-to-eight-year challenge which lie ahead for the fifth president of Gallaudet College will be of assistance to the Board of Trustees and other participants who will be involved in considering candidates for this position. Perhaps some important beliefs, skills, abilities, and attitudes of the next president can be inferred from this perspective. This is, after all, the perspective of an individual who as the incumbent is limited by the fact that he is involved in the daily press of duties. It surely is not the only perspective on this position.

An appendix follows which will present the incumbent president's view of the most immediate agenda for the fifth president of Gallaudet College.

APPENDIX

An Immediate Agenda for the Fifth President of Gallaudet College

The following agenda is presented by the incumbent president of Gallaudet College of more immediate tasks which will be facing the fifth president of the College. Although the major challenges for the next five to eight years have been spelled out previously, these items will need attention reasonably soon.

Presidential Agenda

1. Increasing funding levels, including raising the authorization levels from the federal government.
2. Increasing funding levels from the private sector, including funding from foundations, corporations, and gifts.
3. Establishing the Gallaudet Educational Foundation as a means of attracting major gifts and as a means for managing a growing corpus for the College.
4. Continuing the detailed planning for the influx of students deafened during the rubella epidemic, especially as students complete the preparatory year and enter the main campus.
5. Giving special attention to the adjustment of students at the Northwest campus, including the articulation of activities there with residents in the neighborhood.
6. Ensuring maximum utilization and productivity of resources of the College, including the focusing of resources on the more critical needs of the institution during the years rubella students are enrolled.

7. Providing adequate faculty and support staff during the years of enrollment increases.

8. Obtaining one or two major grants for projects related to the mission of Gallaudet College.

9. Capitalizing on research outcomes, such as cued speech and the autocuer, so that these developments make a positive difference in the lives of deaf people.

10. Seeing positive publicity for the institution so that the general public becomes increasingly aware of the institution.

11. Promoting cooperation and collaboration with other colleges so the expertise and knowledge of Gallaudet College can reach and benefit deaf people of all ages in different geographical sections of the United States.

12. Within three or four years, realizing the mission of Gallaudet College by the establishment of new goals and subsequently restructuring the College and the resources of the institution to achieve these goals.

LETTER FROM DR. EDWARD C. MERRILL TO JANE BASSETT SPILMAN[22]

STONEWOOD
34 Saunooke Road
Asheville, North Carolina
28805

February 26, 1988

Mrs. Jane Bassett Spilman
Chairman
Board of Trustees
Gallaudet University
Washington, D.C.

Dear Mrs. Spilman:

Since concluding my term of office as the fourth President of Gallaudet in October, 1983, I have been gratified with the continued progress of the institution. Dr. Lee has been an astute leader, and the Board of Trustees has acted wisely in supporting his administration. I am writing to you now because I am still deeply interested in Gallaudet University and the clientele it serves.

From my perspective, having purposefully removed myself from the affiars [sic] of the University for the past few years, the University now faces a moment of truth as it always does when a new president must be named. On this occasion, however, the three deaf candidates as well as the hearing candidates are exceptionally well qualified. To what extent, then, is the element of deafness to be weighed in the selection of a president to

---

22. Edward C. Merrill, Letter from Dr. Edward C. Merrill Jr. to Jane Bassett Spilman, February 26, 1988. Courtesy of the personal files of Philip W. Bravin (reprinted with permission from the Merrill family).

serve a deaf student body and a deaf national constituency? Two developments may shed some light on this issue. One development is the historical evolution of social institutions, and the other development is a well established psychological principle that functions in groups and institutions in modern society.

The education of severely handicapped children and youth in the United States was virtually nonexistent until Samuel G. Howe started the first school for the blind and proved, in colaboration [*sic*] with Laura Bridgeman, that blind persons could be educated. Thomas H. Gallaudet, who established the first school for deaf children, made a similar contribution. From these beginnings, the education of handicapped persons has steadily evolved from residential schools to special but separate classes in regular schools, to various forms of integration, to increased integration with the regular school population with special assistance as needed. Although the present pattern of special education provides an important role for special schools, the policy of the nation (expressed, in my opinion, in a very flawed piece of Federal Legislation called, Public Law 94-142, The Education of All Handicapped Children Act of 1975) gives impetus to de-institutionalization. In view of this policy, it is very important that Gallaudet University not be viewed as nor assume the role of an institution in the classical sense that it is an organization headed by an expert who is himself "normal" to provide clinical services (in this case education) to clients who are themselves incapable (disabled) of obtaining the services that are needed. The best way, of course, to insure that Gallaudet is not viewed as an institution is to have as its chief executive officer a person who has overcome the debilitating effects of the disability common among the group that the University purports to serve.

The second development which makes deafness an issue in the naming of the next president is more of a psychological phenomenon rising out of the efforts of minorities to receive fair and equal treatment in the fifites [*sic*] (supported by the Supreme Court decision on Brown v. Board of Education, 1954) and more recently by young people in the sixties in search of relevance in education. The bottom line of all of these developments, much too numerous to mention here, is that the individuals involved were seeking institutions which had credibility in terms which they could accept. In the naming of the seventh president of Gallaudet University, the credibility of the institution is at stake. The Board of Trustees does not control how prospective students, the alumni, the profession, and members of NAD or of NFSD will perceive Gallaudet. Will these persons, the clientel[e] of the institution, see Gallaudet as an institution with a high degree of credibility? With a hearing person as president in the face of qualified deaf candidates, I would say the continued high credibility of the institution is doubtful. With a deaf president, I would say that the credibility of the institution would reach an all-time high. In the latter case, Gallaudet University would have a continued vital role.

Should the element of deafness be considered in the selection of the next president of Gallaudet University? We know that Federal law prohibits discrimination in employment on the basis of a handicapping condition. In view of the special mission of this University, the information presented above argues strongly that candidates who have coped with and largely overcome deafness have an unusual potential for serving the University well.

I trust these observations might be helpful to you and your associates on the Board of Trustees if you care to share them. I am informed enough to know that there are a few members who do not favor a deaf president and who state that it is doubtful that a deaf executive could manage budgetary matters well or could represent the University well in Congressional Hearings.

These arguments are entirely spurious. These persons are probably insecure around deaf persons, and this produces a mind set that makes them overly cautious. We have seen these attitudes before, and we have seen them disappear rapidly as deaf administrators accepted and discharged heavy management responsibilities as deans and vice-presidents in the University.

Thomas Hopkins Gallaudet and Edward Miner Gallaudet were both graduates of Yale University, but Edward Miner's mother had no opportunity to attend any college or university because she was deaf. This was Edward Miner Gallaudet's motivation in establishing a college. As he put it:

> I . . . asked him (his friend, Mr. Ayers) if he did not think it would be possible to develop the proposed school for the deaf at Washington into a college under the patronage of the Federal government.[23]

I am sure that the success of Gallaudet, especially its university status so aptly provided by Dr. Lee and the Congress, would surpass his remotest dreams. He could not imagine the positive impact of the institution he established in opening the doors of education everywhere and at all levels to deaf persons with correlative developments in employment, civic involvement, and even political action. The greatest compliment to him and to those who followed him, including Dr. Lee and me, would be to know that Gallaudet University was still a pioneer in the education of the deaf—under the leadership of a deaf person.

Sincerely yours,
Edward C. Merrill Jr.
President Emeritus
Gallaudet University

---

23. Original handwritten manuscript by Dr. Edward Miner Gallaudet.

ECM: swp

cc: Mr. Gerald Burstein, President
Gallaudet University Alumni Association

Dr. Lawrence Newman, President
National Association of the Deaf

Mr. Robert Anderson, Grand President
National Fraternal Society of the Deaf

Bibliography

Armstrong, David F. "Deaf President Now and the Struggle for Deaf Control of Gallaudet University." *Sign Language Studies* 15, no. 1 (2014): 42–56.

———. *The History of Gallaudet University: 150 Years of a Deaf American Institution.* Washington, DC: Gallaudet University Press, 2014.

Ash, William J. "Who Said What When . . . In Their Own Words." *DCARA News,* April 1988.

Atwood, Albert W. *Gallaudet College, Its First One Hundred Years.* Lancaster, PA: Intelligencer Printing Company, 1964.

Ayres, R. Drummond. "Demonstrations by the Deaf Bring a Resignation But Not Yet a Truce." *New York Times,* March 12, 1988.

Baynton, Douglas C., Jack R. Gannon, and Jean Lindquist Bergey. *Through Deaf Eyes: A Photographic History of an American Community.* Washington, DC: Gallaudet University Press, 2007.

Clinton, William J. "Remarks at the Gallaudet University Commencement Ceremony." Commencement Address, Gallaudet University, Washington, DC, May 14, 1994. https://www.govinfo.gov/content/pkg/PPP-1994-book1/pdf/PPP-1994-book1-doc-pg906.pdf.

Dozier, Jana. "Hear No Evil." *AGB Reports* 30, no. 4 (July/August 1988): 6–18.

Education of the Deaf Act of 1986, S.1874 (1986). https://www.congress.gov/bill/99th-congress/senate-bill/1874.

Gallaudet University. "Deaf President Now." Accessed February 2, 2020, https://www.gallaudet.edu/about/history-and-traditions/deaf-president-now.

———. "In Their Own Words." Accessed February 2, 2020, https://www.gallaudet.edu/about/history-and-traditions/deaf-president-now/profiles-and-viewpoints/in-their-own-words.

———. "Task Force Named to Study Gallaudet University Board." Press release, May 9, 1988.

Gallaudet University Board of Trustees. "Resolution for Year 125." October 1988. Unpublished paper.

Gannon, Jack R. *Deaf Heritage: A Narrative History of Deaf America.* Washington, DC: Gallaudet University Press, 2012.

———. *The Week the World Heard Gallaudet.* Washington, DC: Gallaudet University Press, 1989.

Gilliam, Dorothy. "A President for Gallaudet." *Washington Post*, February 22, 1988.

Harkin, Tom. "Remarks of Senator Tom Harkin, Inauguration of President I. King Jordan." 134 Cong. Rec. pt. 23 (1988): 32597.

———. "Inauguration of I. King Jordan to the Presidency of Gallaudet University." 134 Cong. Rec. pt. 23 (1988): 32596–97.

———. "Harkin Statement on 150th Anniversary of Gallaudet University: The US Senate Committee on Health, Education, Labor & Pensions." April 8, 2014. https://www.help.senate.gov/ranking/newsroom/press/harkin-statement-on-150th-anniversary-of-gallaudet-university.

Johnson, Peter. "Deaf College Vibrates with Victory." *USA Today*, March 14, 1988.

Lane, Harlan. *When the Mind Hears*. New York: Random House, 1984.

Legon, Rick. "The 10 Habits of Highly Effective Boards." *Trusteeship* 22, no. 2 (March/April 2014). https://agb.org/trusteeship-issue/the-10-habits-of-highly-effective-boards-march-april-2014/.

Levesque, Jack. "WOW! What a Ride!" *DCARA News*, April 1988.

Merrill, Edward C. Letter from Dr. Edward C. Merrill Jr. to George Muth. July 15, 1982. Unpublished ms.

———. "Challenges Facing the Fifth President of Gallaudet College." August 1982. Unpublished ms.

———. "The Feasibility of a Deaf Person Serving as President of Gallaudet College." July 7, 1982. Unpublished ms.

Oelsner, Lesley. "Parkinson Denies Knowingly Playing Watergate-Payment Role." *New York Times*, December 19, 1974. https://www.nytimes.com/1974/12/19/archives/parkinson-denies-knowingly-playing-watergatepayment-role-passed-on.html.

Piccoli, Sean. "Gallaudet Rally Calls for Deaf President." *Washington Times*, March 2, 1988.

Sacks, Oliver W. *Seeing Voices: A Journey into the World of the Deaf*. Berkeley: University of California Press, 1989.

———. "The Revolution of the Deaf." *New York Review of Books* 35, no. 9 (June 2, 1988): 23.

Shapiro, Joseph P. *No Pity: People with Disabilities Forging a New Civil Rights Movement*. New York: Times Books, 1994.

Sinclair, Molly. "Gallaudet U. Selects First Deaf President." *Washington Post*, March 14, 1988.

———, and Eric Pianin. "Protest May Imperil Gallaudet Funding." *Washington Post*, March 9, 1988.

Stokoe, Bill. Letter from Bill Stokoe to Phil and Judy Bravin. September 13, 1988. Unpublished paper.

Strauss, Karen Peltz. *A New Civil Right: Telecommunications Equality for Deaf and Hard of Hearing Americans*. Washington, DC: Gallaudet University Press, 2006.

"Thousands Gather for Inauguration Here." *On the Green*, October 31, 1988.

To Amend the Education of the Handicapped Act to Provide Educational Assistance to All Handicapped Children, and For Other Purposes, P.L. 94-142, 89 Stat. 773 (1975).

Williams, Lena. "College for the Deaf Is Shut by Protest Over President." *New York Times*, March 8, 1988.

Zinser, Elisabeth. "Dr. Elisabeth Zinser: Breaking the Silence." *Deaf Life* 5, no. 4 (November 1991).

Zwingle, J. L. "What Boards Can Learn from Gallaudet's Leadership Crisis." *AGB Reports* 30, no. 4 (July/August 1988): 14–15.

About the Author

The Bravin family. Judy and Phil surrounded by (left to right), Seth, Deb, and Jeff.

Philip W. Bravin is currently the vice president of Product Strategy and Innovation at ZVRS/Purple, a video relay company serving the deaf and hard of hearing community since 2008. He has held various positions within the deaf community and in the corporate business community over the years. He stepped down from Communication Service for the Deaf (CSD) in Sioux Falls, SD, in July 2005. At CSD, he held a variety of executive positions in corporate research and development, marketing, broadcasting, and business development, in addition to helping pioneer the development of CSD's video relay service. Prior to joining CSD in 1999, Mr. Bravin was president of Yes You Can, Inc., an organization specializing in enabling people with the latest technological advancements, in addition to providing management, marketing, and technical consulting to schools, nonprofit organizations, and major corporations. He was formerly the president and chief executive officer of the National Captioning Institute (NCI), once the largest provider of closed captioning services in the world, for close to three years, and played a role in formulating the captioning policy that was part of the Telecommunications Act of 1996. Prior to joining NCI, he worked for IBM Corporation for nearly twenty-five years in a variety of technical, marketing, and management positions. He is currently a member and former president of the board of the Lexington School/Center for the Deaf in New York. He served on the board of trustees at Gallaudet University for twenty years, in which capacity he served as chair from 1988 to 1993. He is trustee emeritus of the Gallaudet board. He is the recipient of a doctor of humane letters degree from Gallaudet University. He is often called on to make presentations all over the United States on how technology enhances the lives of people who are deaf and hard of hearing and consults to corporations and organizations from time to time. He is a member of the National Association of the Deaf and other organizations. He is a co-patent holder for Patent No. 7333507 for a multimodal communications system, which was awarded in 2008. Privately, he loves to tinker with his computers and model trains, and grabs every opportunity to snowshoe and hike with his wife. Residing in Chester, Vermont, he is married to Judith Bravin, a retired librarian at the New York School for the Deaf, father of three grown deaf children, and grandfather of twelve grandchildren.

My (legally) custom-made New York license plates, which I used for years after DPN until we moved to South Dakota in 2003.